T0161774

Diary of Bergen-Belsen

Diary of Bergen-Belsen

Hanna Lévy-Hass

Translated by Sophie Hand
With an Introduction and Afterword by Amira Hass

First self-published in 1946 in Yugoslavia. First published in book form by FIR in French and German in 1961. First published in English in 1982 by Harvester Books/Barnes & Noble.

This edition published in 2009 by Haymarket Books
P.O. Box 180165, Chicago, IL 60618
773-583-7884
info@haymarketbooks.org
www.haymarketbooks.org

Trade distribution:
In the U.S., Consortium Book Sales, www.cbsd.com
In the UK, Turnaround Publisher Services, www.turnaround-psl.com

This book was published with the generous support of Lannan Foundation and the Wallace Action Fund.

Cover design by Eric Ruder

Library of Congress Cataloguing in Publication Data
Lévy-Hass, Hanna.
[Vielleicht war das alles erst der Anfang. English]
Diary of Bergen Belsen / Hanna Levy-Hass ; introduction and afterword by Amira Hass.
p. cm.
ISBN 978-1-60846-460-9 (paperback)
1. Bergen-Belsen (Concentration camp) 2. Holocaust, Jewish (1939-1945)--Personal narratives. I. Hass, Amira. II. Title.
D805.G3L4213 2007
940.53'18092--dc22
[B]
2007034807

2 4 6 8 10 9 7 5 3 1

Printed in Canada

Contents

For Eike Geisel,
June 1, 1945–August 6, 1997

—Amira Hass

Notes on My Mother

Hanna Lévy-Hass
Born in Sarajevo, March 18, 1913
Died in Jerusalem, June 10, 2001

In the latter half of the 1980s, Hanna Lévy-Hass considered the possibility of going back and resettling in her homeland, Yugoslavia. She was already seventy-five years old. Five years earlier, she packed a suitcase, picked up her walking stick, which had become increasingly necessary, left her room and books in Tel Aviv and took off, heading to Geneva and later Paris.

No specific destination, no explicit duration. During her wanderings she visited Belgrade where, fifty years earlier, she had studied at the university. In 1945, after surviving Bergen-Belsen, she returned to Belgrade, intending to stay for good.

This introductory text was originaly written for the Spanish edition of *Diary of Bergen-Belsen*.

She was born in 1913 in Sarajevo, but Belgrade had been imprinted in her memory as a more modern city, worthy of her second return in the late 1980s. She nearly rented a room in some apartment, ready to start her life over again. The landlady watched her peer out the window. She knew her prospective tenant was Jewish, and chose to tell her that "Here, out of this window, we watched how the Jews were rounded up." This alone prompted my mother to give up the idea of renting that room, and, furthermore, made her realize that Belgrade was not for her.

This strikes me as rather strange. Did my mother actually need that Belgrade woman to make her insensitive comment in order to realize that through the windows of many houses people watched Jews being rounded up and taken away to an unknown destination during the German occupation of the city? Do such "windows" not exist in other European capitals as well? After all, the German occupation forces and their indigenous collaborators rounded up Jews and sent them away—regardless of the windows through which they were watched, or not.

◆ ◆ ◆

This was so characteristic of her, as I knew her: to travel from Paris to Belgrade and give up her homecoming at the strike of an insensitive comment.

This was her restlessness, her impulsive nature, even as she faced increasing difficulty in walking. It was the need to relocate, to leave, to change her mind and leave again—actually, to run away. And when, in the early 1990s, she decided to leave France, where she had almost settled, and go back to Israel—this too was a sort of feverish escape. Again she found herself an outsider.

Had she always been this way? I mean, was she like this before shipment—for being a Jew—to the Nazi concentration camp of Bergen-Belsen? This is just one of the many questions that make up her biography.

The biographical bits and pieces that I know (and remember) about her are proof, nevertheless, of the stability and determination of her choices as a young woman. When her female peers normally opted for the traditional anchor of marriage and raising a family, my mother chose higher education as a matter of course: studying Latin languages (especially French and Italian) and literature. She prepared herself to be a teacher, even began her graduate studies.

She studied in Belgrade, where she moved with her mother and one sister in the early 1930s. State scholarships enabled her to study, a blessing for the daughter of a non-wealthy family impoverished by the late 1920s world economic crisis. She was also awarded a scholarship for several months of study at the Sorbonne in Paris.

She was born just before World War I broke out, in Sarajevo, Bosnia: a godforsaken corner of the Austro-Hungarian Empire. A classmate of her brother's—twenty years her elder—one Gavrilo Princip, a Serb nationalist activist, assassinated the Austrian heir to the throne in Sarajevo on June 28, 1914. A month later, Austria-

Hungary declared war on Serbia. She did not say much about her experience of those first war years. Like millions of others, the family suffered hunger, which especially affected her—the baby—and her future health.

She was the youngest daughter in a family of Sephardic Jews. She had three brothers and four sisters. The family tree, like that of other families in the Balkans, reaches back to Spain, from which they were expelled by the Catholic kingdoms of Aragon and Castilla at the end of the fifteenth century.

The language spoken at home was Ladino—fifteenth-century Spanish mixed with early Hebrew. Religious ceremonies were conducted in Ladino. Family songs were sung in Ladino. Hana—called Anica by her family—understood Ladino, but spoke Serbo-Croat. "Goya," her father teased her, for not answering in her mother tongue, that medieval Spanish spiced with Hebrew.

Ladino, Serbo-Croat, mother tongue—how confusing ... I always knew she spoke "Yugoslav." That is how we referred to her language, orally, briefly, and comfortably.

As the war ended in German-Austrian defeat, Bosnia became a part of the Kingdom of Yugoslavia. A common joke says the only "Yugoslavs" were the Jews: neither Bosnian, nor Serb, nor Croatian. The Jews were at ease with the new federation, a mixture of religious and ethnic identities under one regime. Perhaps they were at ease with the nonethnic, egalitarian potential of a federation where their Jewishness was but one piece—neither inferior nor su-

perior—of a richly colorful mosaic. Such, in any case, was my
mother's regard for her homeland: she was born in Bosnia, studied
in Serbia, read and wrote both Latin and Cyrillic, and had friends
of all ethnicities and religious backgrounds. She felt equal among
equals. Her brothers and sisters were scattered among the various
republics. Especially in the communist underground with which
she was affiliated as a young woman, this mixture was natural.

In those years, people like her, many of them Jews, sought
anything that crossed national, ethnic, and religious borders.
They were united by the ideal of equality. People around her as a
matter of course joined the international brigades fighting against
the fascists in the Spanish civil war. Among them was a Jewish
youngster with whom a budding love had begun to form. I no
longer know his name. I only "remember," through her stories,
that he was a redhead, and that he was killed on Spanish soil.

Hostilities and tensions among the various groups in Yugoslavia in the 1920s and '30s intensified and became full-blown
inner strife under the Nazi occupation and alongside the Resistance. These, however, did not really surface in the memories she
left me as her legacy. Perhaps her Bergen-Belsen experience, and
the fact that so many of her relatives and friends perished, shut out
the severity of other memories. Perhaps those hostilities,
pre–World War II, were less severe than we interpret them in ret-
rospect, from our vantage point after the civil wars that tore Yugoslavia apart at the end of the twentieth century. And perhaps in
spite of her later political disenchantments, she preserved some of

that popular communist romanticism that presented hostilities as a binary phenomenon of good and bad guys: monarchy versus the people, Fascists (Croats) versus anti-Nazis, treacherous monarchists versus partisans and communists. And perhaps these distant complexities just weren't the right stuff for my childhood stories.

Either way, my mother definitely regarded Yugoslavia as her homeland, its songs as her songs, and its landscape as her own. Her oldest brother, Mihael, was a well-known Zionist activist, whereas nothing was further from her mind than migrating to that far-off land of Palestine—not prior to 1945, nor when she came back from Bergen-Belsen in the summer of 1945. Nor did she consider emigrating anywhere else, as other Jews had, the few who had survived. Her sister, Cilika, for example, left for the United States. But Hanna Lévy wanted to stay, grow new roots, and help build the "new Yugoslavia." And here is another of those questions that make up her biography: How did she eventually find herself a citizen of the new state, Israel?

A mere five years before liberation she had left Belgrade for a teaching position in Montenegro: as a Jew, in a monarchy that wished to please Nazi-ruled Germany, she could not find work in the "metropolis," only in the suburbs. She parted with her mother at the Belgrade train station, and commented to me curtly, years later, that she knew it would be their last meeting. From the silence that always accompanied this statement, I know it was one of the most painful memories she bore. As a child, I thought she told me a lot about her past. I thought I knew everything about her and the family. Now I know that silences were a substantial and weighty component of her biography—far more so than the details she told me and the details I recall.

In 1940, she could not possibly have known that within a year she would find herself under the relatively "light" Italian occupation. Her family, however, split among Belgrade and Sarajevo (where her father, two sisters and their families, and elder brother and his family were still living) and Croatia (another sister and brother), immediately experienced far worse occupation and persecution. This persecution reached her only in September 1943, as Italy surrendered and the territories it ruled were taken over by Germany. She was about to join the partisans, with whom she was in contact under Italian occupation—she had already taken part in one of the battles—as a paramedic. She never hid from me how frightened to death she was from the shooting. Once the Germans took over, she failed to persuade the small Jewish community in Danilovgrad, the small town where she taught, to join her. As she finished packing and was about to take off for "the mountains," three young Jews appeared in her rented room and begged her to stay. They were convinced that the Germans would soon learn of her absence, realize she joined the partisans, and, in retaliation, murder the remaining members of the community—about thirty individuals. In late 1943 people knew well enough that Nazi Germany was murdering Jews wherever it ruled. Still, Hanna Lévy, a thirty-year-old woman, could not ignore the request of the small community's representatives. She could not bear to ask herself, afterward, whether she had been instrumental to their deaths. For her, joining the partisans did not necessarily mean "saving herself" or "survival." Death was more likely than survival. The question only remained how a Jew like her would die.

She stayed with the Jews, and with them she was eventually arrested (February 1944) and imprisoned for six months by the Gestapo at Cetinje, Montenegro. There, too, she kept a diary. This she told Eike Geisel, a German researcher, publicist, and left-wing activist, who in the late 1970s "discovered" her Bergen-Belsen diary. Until then it had not been circulated beyond communist circles in Israel and Europe. Geisel decided to introduce it to the German public. His interview with her followed the publication of her diary by Rotbuch Verlag, a German publishing house with which Geisel was associated. I, for one, have no recollection of her ever telling me of a diary she kept at the Gestapo jail, an act that—as she told Geisel—was even more of a risk than writing a diary in Bergen-Belsen, as the jail was small and the prisoners under close and constant observation. Clearly, this diary was lost, which is not surprising considering her later wanderings. Surprising, though, is the minimal importance she attributed to herself and her own writing, as she obviously felt no need to tell me about it. And perhaps the reason lies not in underestimating herself but, again, in choosing to remain silent. But why? That is another biographical question.

She volunteered very little information about prison. Once I asked her whether the Germans tortured them—her—there. She said they did not. I wanted and still want to hope that is true. She said that because of the partisans' close presence, the Germans did not dare hurt the detainees. Their families actually approached the prison gate and delivered food packages and personal messages. Still, the Germans did murder prisoners. She told me of one execution, of a prisoner who was the wife of a partisan leader. The guards dragged her off to the gallows. She resisted, shouted, begged for her life. Her shouts were unbearable. One of the other women prisoners could no longer stand it. In spite of her mates' protests, she helped the guards drag the condemned woman away in order to end everyone's torment. For my mother this became—as she would tell me years later—an example of collaboration, the memory of which would always produce a shiver of revulsion.

At some point, in June or July 1944, the meticulous Nazi killing industry separated the non-Jews from the Jews in that Gestapo jail. The former remained incarcerated, while the latter were loaded onto freight trains headed for an unknown—but obvious—destination. Germany was sustaining defeats on its various fronts, but clung doggedly to its mission of wiping the Jews off the face of the earth. Those who "merely obeyed orders" made no attempt to conceal this.

A friend of my mother's—a gentile Montenegran—came to the spot where Jews were being assembled. She approached the Germans (as my mother told Eike Geisel) and announced that she wished give something to Fräulein Lévy. The two of them had agreed earlier that my mother would entrust her with documents, including her various diplomas. "What is this?" shouted the German soldier. "Papers she will need later on. I'll keep them for her," answered the woman (unfortunately my mother did not recall her name). "You really think you'll ever come back?" the soldier shouted at my mother. "Why do you need these things?" My mother still handed her friend the papers, and he began to yell again: "You'll never come back. What do you care about those papers?"

War and front-line considerations probably kept the Germans from transporting the remaining Jews all the way from Montenegro to one of the murder camps in Poland. According to one of the rumors that my mother heard, the murder of this tiny group of Jews was supposed to be carried out in Belgrade or at the Yugoslav border. When this was not done, they were sent to Bergen-Belsen concentration camp in the north of Germany.

Instead of the prisoners-of-war camp at Bergen-Belsen, which was not filled to capacity, a detention camp for Jews was created in April 1943 to incarcerate Jews who were also British or American subjects and might eventually be exchanged for Germans imprisoned in Britain or the United States. The exchange plan was contrived by the legal department of the German foreign ministry. Thus the camp was defined as an *Aufenthaltslager*, a detention camp where conditions would not result in certain death, as they did in other concentration camps. But for about 1,700 of the 2,500 "exchangeable Jews" who first arrived there in mid-July 1943, the camp was a mere transit stop on the way to the Auschwitz death camp. These were Polish Jews holding South American citizenship papers, the validity of which the German authorities had chosen not to honor. During the first half of 1944, only about 350 of the initial Polish-Jewish group (those whom the Germans acknowledged as "exchangeable") remained in Bergen-Belsen.

In mid-August 1943, a transport delivered 441 Jews from Thessaloniki to Bergen-Belsen, seventy-four of whom were officially recognized Greek Jews, and the rest were *Spanioles*— Sephardic Jews who had resided in Greece for a long time but retained their Spanish citizenship. This spared them the fate suffered by the rest of Thessaloniki's Jews—forty-six thousand—nearly all of whom were sent to the Auschwitz gas chambers. Following negotiations between the Spanish government and the German foreign ministry, the fortunates were sent to Spain in early February 1944, and then on to a detention camp in North Africa. From there they eventually emigrated to Palestine. Shortly after their departure from Bergen-Belsen, another group of Spanish and Portuguese Jews arrived. 155 Spanish Jews and nineteen Portugese Jews had been arrested as part of an extensive Jew-hunt in Athens, which was occupied by German forces in late March 1944. Unlike the rest of the Jews of Greece and Italy, who were caught and freighted to Auschwitz, citizens of the Iberian Peninsula were taken to Bergen-Belsen after a fortnight on the trains. They were situated in the "neutrals" encampment (a part of the camp originally destined for neutral nationals), and there they remained until the end of the war.

As of early 1944, the largest group of "exchangeables" in the camp consisted of Dutch Jews—3,670 in all. From January 1, 1944, until July of that year, the number of "exchangeable" Jews grew from 379 to 4,100. However, in March 1944 the camp was transformed from a "detention camp" into a "concentration camp"—another link in the murderous assembly line that sought to add more and more numbers to its death production toll. In any case, "exchangeable" Jews were kept in a separate area of the camp. Unlike "orderly" extermination camps such as Auschwitz, where the killing was methodical, Bergen-Belsen produced death by means of terrible crowding, starvation, thirst, illness, epidemics, and the absence of any sanitation.

Conditions at the camp had worsened by the time Hanna Lévy arrived in summer 1944. By January 1945, conditions were rapidly deteriorating under the command of Josef Kramer. Between January and mid-April 1945, nearly thirty-five thousand people had died there—18,168 of them in March alone. Another fourteen thousand died between the camp's liberation date, April 15, and June 20.

Countless bodies were heaped in piles throughout the camp. About four days before its liberation by the British army, camp authorities forced inmates—the ones who still stood on their own feet and resembled walking skeletons—to dig huge pits outside the camp fences and dump the bodies there. The inmates, in teams of four, were required to drag each body by means of cloth or leather strapped to the ankles and armpits. Under the watchful eyes of SS guards and the whiplashes of the *Kapos* (inmates-in-charge, usually criminal prisoners), about two thousand living skeletons buried the dead to the strains of incessant dance music played by two prisoner orchestras.

The British, whose charge of the camp was established by an armistice agreement with the local German Army commander, had no notion of what they would find at the camp: piles of bodies in various states of decay, sewage ditches filled with corpses, still-breathing skeletons lying next to the already dead on bunks in the barracks, hastily filled burial pits. Behind the camp an open pit was found, partly filled with bodies. The barracks, each meant to house about one hundred human beings, were crammed with six hundred to one thousand people.

But my mother was no longer there. Another of the death industry's caprices: between April 6 and 11, about seven thousand Jews were loaded onto three trains destined for Theresienstadt, Czechoslovakia. My mother was on one of these, ill with typhus like all the others. This is what she told Geisel:

> We were no longer fully conscious of what was happening—everything was hazy. Sometimes we were allowed to get out of the cars, and since the Germans themselves did not really know what to expect, the guards did not watch us too closely. We used to scramble down the railway embankment and pick blades of grass, which we boiled and ate. We were at the end of our tether, and our bodies were like skeletons.

The train moved on. Many died inside its cars and occasionally the bodies were hurled out. Out of the fog in which everyone found themselves, the living would occasionally disembark to dig for potatoes, which they knew the Germans had stored under piles of soil. When the less weak dug and found some, others pounced on the potatoes. Then the German soldiers burst into this starved crowd and trampled everyone with their boots, beating up whoever held onto a potato. At one stop, some Yugoslav prisoners of war, who were working in one of the villages nearby, showed up. They yelled in Yugoslav: "Tu Jugoslovena ima li?" (Are there any Yugoslavs here?) Not "Serbs," not "Bosnians," not "Croats." "Yugoslavs." How wonderful it sounded, that simple phrase. My mother and a few of her fellow Yugoslavs responded immediately. But they noticed that their countrymen turned their eyes away, afraid to direct their gaze at the emaciated figures. Eyes averted, the Yugoslavs invited them to come along and take a few potatoes. Only my mother and another young woman felt strong enough for the trek—two or three kilometers—to gather potatoes for themselves and the others.

Returning with a whole sack of potatoes on her back—she had no idea where she found the energy to haul it—she discovered to her surprise that the other young woman had vanished and their train was gone. She was all alone. As a young girl, I loved listening to her tell how she hid behind some bushes and watched the soldiers of the glorious German Army run for their lives, away from the approaching Red Army. But I do not know if that happened on the same night or later.

That night she went back to the village where the prisoners of war had been working and to the farm where she had gathered the potatoes. Over the town hall a white flag was already waving, although the Red Army had not yet arrived. My mother said she feared the woman: afraid of her revulsion at seeing someone who "no longer looked human"—a filthy skeleton crawling with lice. The woman invited her to stay the night, but my mother preferred to sleep in the barn or cowshed. She did not know what the woman would do, or what her chances were to stay alive. "I was like a terrified beast." But the next day, some soldiers of the Red Army occupied the village: nothing more was needed, for no one in the village fired a shot or offered any resistance. She heard soldiers speaking Russian and joyously ran toward them. They yelled at her to keep her distance, not realizing she was one of the few in the village who felt "liberated" rather than "occupied." In her ears, even their shouts rang like divine singing.

This all happened before Germany officially surrendered on May 8. Hanna Lévy spent some weeks wandering along roads filled with people just like her, of all nationalities, liberated prisoners of war and other types of prisoners, all homeward bound: to Russia, Italy, Greece, Bulgaria, Czechoslovakia, Poland, Yugoslavia, some on foot, others on carts, but most walking. Once she found a group of Italians who had been taken captive and sent to German labor camps, and, feeling safe with them, joined them for quite a stretch of the way. Speaking no language but Italian, they welcomed her fluency in German and Italian. They obtained food, clothes, and nightly shelter in villages. She spared no words to describe the pleasure of their company. "Communists, workers, good people," she described them to Geisel in the late 1970s. "Bit by bit I began to look human again," due to food, showers, rest, freedom.

She then began to pick up the pieces of her life, and the mission seemed possible thanks to her firm conviction that barbarism must be replaced by a totally different and new era of civilization. An important component of this new civilization, whose outline was still rather vague, was the emergence of transnational and nonreligious identities based on the common denominator of the ideology of equality and the common rejection of any form of hierarchy and discrimination: economic, national, or religious. Thus, the company of these Italians was so natural and good for her, and as such it etched itself in her memory.

◆ ◆ ◆

They walked most of the way to Dresden. There, after a break in their trek, they stole a train. That was the advice they had received upon asking how to get out of the ruined city, how to escape from the Germans, whose sense of victimhood—not their national affiliation, not even the question as to what they had done and what they had known—struck my mother, and kept her at a distance. "Steal a train," people said. "That is the only way to get home." And so they did. They found a train car, attached to it a steam engine headed for the border, and off they went.

I do not recall hearing from her, when I was a child, about this train theft. I learned of it only much later, in the interview with Geisel. But this is exactly the kind of story she liked telling me, and the kind I loved hearing: a mischievous tale that evokes a smile, that begs knowing all the details, a vignette befitting an Italian film. And I had thought her many silences contained just all the unbearable, inconceivable thoughts and specifics. Such as how her mother, Rifka, and sister, Rosa, were taken away from their home in Belgrade.

She once blurted a few words about how—when she came back to Belgrade—neighbors told her how her mother and sister had been dragged out of the house by Nazi police or by Croatian fascists; I no longer know which. She told me clearly, during my childhood, that she would not repeat what she was told. This was, in other words, her declared intention to keep silent. According to information she eventually received, they were both murdered in Auschwitz. Only a few years ago, after my mother's death, did I learn from her 1921-born nephew Jasha that it was not in Auschwitz but rather on Yugoslav soil that they were murdered, choked to death in a truck. In spring 1942, Jews—especially women and children—who were kept in a detention camp near Belgrade (most Jewish men had already been murdered one way or another) were loaded onto trucks. The children were offered sweets and adults were told they were to be relocated, no longer to suffer hunger or cold. Exhaust pipes from the engine were routed into the cabins and the trucks drove and drove until they arrived with their dead cargo at pits that had been dug in advance.

My mother also kept her silence about the fate of the rest of her family—her father, Yakov and other sister, Serafina (along with her husband Mauricio and son Marcelo); and another brother, Braco, who lived in Zagreb: her father starved to death in his hideout in Sarajevo; her sister, brother-in-law, and nephew were caught and sent to one of the stations of the death industry. Her brother, a lawyer in Zagreb, was shot to death early in 1941, having been active in a Jewish resistance group.

A few members of the family survived: the eldest brother, Mihael, whom the Italians had caught and exiled along with his wife Rosa and son Jasha to a detention camp in Italy, which actually saved their lives; a sister, Erna, who was married to a Catholic Croat in Sarajevo (she was the one who eventually told me about the fate of some of our murdered family members); and a sister, Cilika, who had emigrated to the United States.

The untold story of how her mother and sister were taken away explains perhaps why my mother did not insist on repossessing the home that had been their property. By law she was entitled to evict the tenants who lived in it during the war, but she declined this legal fight and gave up the home itself with its empty rooms. Her family had been murdered—would she now make an issue of four walls? Property had no priority for her as she began putting the pieces of her life back together. Work did. She had hoped to resume teaching but was asked to work for the new Yugoslav government, supervising the French broadcasts of Radio Belgrade. Later she was moved to the governmental office, where she translated into French various official documents and publications. These positions guaranteed her wages, stability, social status.

For three years she experienced economic security. Then, contrary to all her expectations of herself, contrary to all her plans, in late 1948 she migrated to Israel, about half a year after the state was founded. Why? Here is the explanation I formulated over the years, having followed my mother as a child, as an adolescent, and finally as an adult, this question always hovering in the background.

During those three years in liberated Belgrade she realized that putting the pieces back together was not merely more difficult than she had imagined, but rather it was impossible. Yugoslavs, on the whole, paid a heavy price for the war and the struggle against their Nazi occupiers. At first glance one would think everyone was similarly busy reconstructing their lives. But soon enough, a great difference became obvious between the fate of Jews under the occupation, and that of non-Jews (except for the Roma, who were murdered in a fashion similar to the Jews).

An entire community had been erased, whole families wiped out, a centuries-old culture gone up in smoke with full intention. For the Slavic nations, the Nazis had planned inferior status, that of slaves in their future racist "new world," but they did not act to exterminate them. The various modes of murder that the Germans exercised clearly differentiated among national groups. To her dismay, she discovered that these differentiations persisted.

Here and there, among her former schoolmates and their families whom she met upon her return, she felt a sort of wariness or impatience with what she had experienced as a Jew. But of that, too, she did not speak much to me—an occasional sentence, as though outlining a sketch. She printed the diary she had written in a tiny notebook in Bergen-Belsen and distributed it. She realized people were not overwhelmed or even interested. They advised her to look ahead, toward the future. Not to dwell on the past. And under the glorified Yugoslav partisans' post-liberation myth, whoever did not take active part in their fight but was "merely captive" did not deserve any special attention.

Not only in Yugoslavia, but also in other European societies that had borne several years of the Nazi yoke, a generation grew up internalizing some of the anti-Semitic Nazi ideology. The Jews who came back felt this soon enough. A young clerk—I no longer recall whether at the population registration bureau that my mother visited upon her return, or at some other public office—said to my mother, genuinely bewildered, "But you are a guest in Yugoslavia!" (meaning "What are you doing here? You do not belong here. You are here temporarily.") Had this been a single foolish outburst, I suppose it would not have offended my mother the way it did. But gradually she realized she was facing an enormous void, made up not only of her own personal and collective bereavement, but also of people's refusal to acknowledge the uniqueness of Jewish-European loss.

And this is the answer to the two biographical questions I raised earlier: this painful tension—between her feelings and experiences as a Yugoslav, a Jew, and a communist (essentially, one who cares deeply and attributes prime importance to any liberation struggle) and the lack of political and emotional acknowledgment of her own personal as well as collective grief—sowed in her the seeds of restlessness that would manifest itself first in her emigration to Israel and later in her various "escapes" (as she herself called them) from Israel for varying lengths of time.

In Yugoslavia this tension appeared politically as well in the power struggle between Tito and Stalin. The Soviet Union supported the founding of the Jewish state. Yugoslavia did not. Soviet foreign minister Andrei Gromyko delivered a quasi-Zionist speech at the United Nations, and linked the founding of the state directly to the Holocaust. This was a liberating speech for many Jewish communists. It solved for them the contradiction between their experience as Jews and the ideological discipline that forced them to minimize the historical significance of that same experience. This was the same discrepancy between seeing Israel as a part of an "imperialist project"—the analysis Hanna Lévy heard from her friends and acquaintances, which on principle she tended to accept—and the understanding that Israel had become the refuge and personal rehabilitation for those whom Europe had rejected in so brutal a fashion.

Then, in Israel she would rediscover how loss and bereavement had not vanished, could not be swept away. That perhaps there were no pieces to put back together, but their absence was indeed a constant in this new life. In Israel, too, she faced alienation and exclusion: in its early years, the Zionist ethos had no sympathy for the diaspora Jews who had "gone like lambs to the slaughter," as it were. The "new Jew" preferred to present the founding of the state as a "resurrection after the Holocaust." This contradicted and silenced the survivors' initial sense that the Holocaust was not something that had an end and was somehow "resurrectable."

In those first years it seemed that activism in the Israeli Communist Party, which Hanna joined as soon as she stepped onto Haifa's shore on December 31, 1948, would resolve discrepancies. Holding onto the utopian vision, the belief that the socialist revolution was on its way, incessant activism with this vision, this faith (writing on behalf of the party, translating, distributing newspapers and pamphlets, demonstrating, holding meetings)—all these alleviated her grief somewhat, filled the constant void she felt in her heart, numbed the sense of a vacuum. No, this was not a conscious, pragmatic choice for therapeutic reasons. Actions toward a meaningful, purposeful future of just relations among humans compensated for the incessant feelings of senselessness and pointlessness that were born of personal and mass bereavement, death, and sporadic survival experienced by her and people like her.

For her this meant choosing a life of dissidence, of constant opposition to the Israeli government and zionist ethos. But this was no easy choice, either socially or economically. Because of her communist activism, for instance, she could not be employed as a teacher in Israel in the 1950s. Her dissidence (and the personal sacrifices it entailed) and utopian belief in the possibility of a different future were perhaps factors that kept her from admitting sooner than she did the oppressive nature of "socialism on earth."

She did not seek extenuating circumstances for her choices. "I am not convinced," she said two or three years before she died, "that I can define myself as a communist." ("Communist" had long ceased to be her party affiliation, and she had not been a party member since the early 1970s). Today I understand her to have meant the quasi-religious rigidity, the lack of any doubt, the messianic faith in a "happy ending" doctrine posing as an "exact science," the fear of contradicting the "leaders," and especially the suppression of information about the goings-on in the "socialist" countries. But she did not become a faithless cynic.

From the early 1970s on, she gave up her Communist Party activism for feminist activism, which was then making its first inroads in Israel. Her early attraction to socialist feminism, and her resentment of male dominance in the Left as well, equipped her to begin to ask questions about so-called socialist regimes.

Feminist activism made her feel at home, even if for a short time, in other places where she tried to settle down. In late 1982, nearing seventy years old, she packed her suitcase, picked up a few books and her walking stick, and went wandering in Europe. The date is no coincidence, although I am not certain she was conscious of its relevance at the time: It was shortly after the massacres in the Palestinian refugee camps of Sabra and Shatila (September 1982). The massacre itself was carried out by the Lebanese Christian Phalanges, but these acted under the watchful eye, inspiration, and protection of the Israeli Army that on June 5, 1982, opened an all-out war against the Palestinians in Lebanon. All the antiwar demonstrations in which she took part, all the interviews she gave, all the pamphlets she handed out, which were signed by her group of survivors and ex-fighters and which demanded a halt to the merchandising of the Holocaust (the Israeli government then compared Yasser Arafat to Hitler in order to justify the war)—only increased her feelings of helplessness and collaboration with oppression done in her name.

A year or two before her death, and several years after a cruel civil war tore apart her Yugoslavia, she summed up her life to me: "All my worlds have been destroyed."

She spoke in telegrams, and when these are unraveled, they reveal a considerable piece of the twentieth century, not only of her own lifetime: "the Jewish community, socialism, Yugoslavia, and Israel." Namely: Jewish life in the diaspora, her own life as a member of the (Sephardic) Jewish minority in Europe, had always seemed natural to her. The Third Reich's new world order put an end to that life. She, after all, had believed that history, people's will, and their conscious action would lead to a just social system, socialism. This faith—a world in itself—was shattered long before the breakdown of the USSR. The dismantling of Yugoslavia and the cruel war it experienced were inconceivable to her own humanist rationalism that had survived Bergen-Belsen, to the extent that she could no longer even listen to Balkan folk songs. She would not be interviewed about the Sarajevo of her childhood. And Israel—her home after 1949, although she had never been nor did she become a Zionist—proved true the warnings she had heard in Yugoslavia prior to her emigration. "This is colonialism," friends told her, trying to disuade her: "What will you do there?"

She did not commit this telegraphic summary of her life to writing. The latter forty years of her life were wrapped in silence, despite her writing talents. Vain were my attempts—as well as those of a young friend of hers, Tirza Waisel, who adopted her as her mentor—to make her speak, to unfold an orderly biography and record her memoirs.

She wrote her diary in Bergen-Belsen while she still had hope for a better world, eventually. Her writing had meaning—documenting and memory had a role in building a world "that will be good." Her silence afterward was an ongoing admission that the postwar world was not new.

Amira Hass
Translated by Tal Haran

Information about Bergen-Belsen was taken from the book *Bergen-Belsen, 1943 bis 1945* by Eberhard Kolb (Göttingen: Bergen Sammlung Vandenhoeck, 1985).

Diary of
Bergen-Belsen

1

My whole being seems paralyzed and with each passing day I feel more apathetic about the world outside, less suited to life as it is now. If our goals and political aims don't materialize, if the world remains as it is now, if new social relations don't emerge and substantially change human nature—well, then, I will finally become and forever remain a clumsy, incompetent, damned creature, a failure.

Up to now I have frequently—even constantly—looked inside myself to find the causes of my misery and unhappiness—in my being, my character, my background. I've always struggled to understand the necessity behind human destiny, individual fate, and to explain such things in light of atavism, heredity, education, childhood, and any number of psychological factors. And I've done the

37

same to understand and explain my own life. The method is sound, no doubt.

But recently it's becoming clearer to me that one's faults aren't something to look for solely in oneself or in one's personal life; they are largely hidden in the world around us. Today, I understand quite well that the endless string of bad days, the dark thoughts, and the extremely difficult situations I've lived through in my life were directly caused by none other than external vicissitudes, the absurdity of the current social structure, and human nature as it is today.

This becomes glaringly obvious today, right here, in this camp, and in the atrocious servitude that binds us to each other. And so I've learned to link my own particular destiny closely to the more general question that will determine the outcome to the current social and international upheaval, and I've learned to envision the solution to my own personal problems, above and beyond all else, within the context of the solution to global problems. So I've decided to stop being the victim of my previous convictions, to free myself from the clutches of individual fatalism that used to throw me defenselessly into an imminent, inevitable, predestined, eternal, and necessarily fatal unhappiness. It goes without saying that in spite of everything, my personal unhappiness flows from these kinds of things, in a sense; but that unhappiness is not a definitive and stable feature, since it *must*, since it can't *not* vary within the general context of the social and global transformations taking place today.

B. B. | August 19, 1944

People from different social classes are crammed together here, but it's the standard petty-bourgeois type that predominates. There are also a few typical capitalist individuals, moderately decadent types. In general, everyone continues to display mean and petty habits, selfishness, and narrow-mindedness. Out of this come endless conflicts of interest, friction, and cases of bigotry on top of it all.

The atmosphere is suffocating. The fact that we were all deported here from every corner of the world and that you hear no fewer than twenty-five languages being spoken is not the worst of it. If only we were united by one determined, common consciousness! But this is not the case. This human mass is heterogeneous. It is piled together here, by force, by violence, in this small patch of dirty, humid ground, forced to live in the most humiliating conditions and to endure the most brutal deprivations, such that all human passions and weaknesses have unleashed themselves, sometimes taking on beastly forms.

What a disgrace! What a sad spectacle! A common misery uniting beings who barely tolerate each other and who add their own lack of social consciousness, mental blindness, as well as those incurable ills of isolated souls, to these distressing objective conditions. Certain selfish instincts have found in this place an ideal ground for their own justification to the point of being grotesque. Nonetheless, it would be wrong to generalize all these problems. But the high moral values that you can sense in some people, their moral and intellectual honesty, remain in the shadows, powerless.

B. B. | August 20, 1944

I feel extremely tired and disconnected from everything around me. My soul moans, aches. Where is beauty hiding? And truth? And love? Oh, how the thought of my life, my whole life, pains me.

B. B. | August 22, 1944

The very limited space and the even more limited possibilities of keeping it clean—it's enough to push anyone to the brink. Rainy days transform the entire space into a mud pit, which further increases the overall level of filth as well as the vermin. And it's all accompanied by interminable squabbles systematically encouraged by the common enemy, the Nazi. It's only the first month and already, depressed, we can foresee endless misery.

I should have gone "up there," into the mountains, to be with them.* Definitely. Of course, there too, over time, you would have noticed some conflicts, some petty disagreements, some minor inconsistencies in some people, a lack of conviction or principles in others ... and it would have been even more painful, more bit-

---

* That is, the Yugoslavian partisans. (H. L.-H.)

ter, perhaps. But at least you would feel like a human being, free to think, to express yourself, to act. And you would be surrounded by human beings, by real men, who say human things to you, men who, today, are the only ones who deserve respect and whose words and deeds matter. Only "up there" could I know my reason for being, my true worth, and what I am truly capable of contributing, or not contributing.

Only there does suffering have meaning. Only there do faults become more obvious and easier to correct. Only there does man learn to know himself and to devote himself. And to the extent that, there too, the verdict would indicate that I am a failure … It would only be for the better. Everything would be clearer: the only thing left for you now is to drop, like an overripe fruit that decomposes of its own accord. Why not? Such is the world. But I suspect vaguely, yet deep within me, that once "up there," I would not necessarily have been destined to total ruin.

Maybe it's precisely this dilemma that landed me here in this wretched camp; it's been tormenting me for some time. On the other hand, because of it many things within me and in others have been clarified. And today I can state without fear of inaccuracy that I was made—if not absolutely then decisively—to be there with them, rather than here. In a sense, this evolution hasn't been totally worthless to me: I came out of it hardened in my convictions, having gotten to know the enemy better and having learned more thoroughly what we must fight in the future. The knowledge acquired was worth it.

B. B. | August 23, 1944

That's not entirely true. I had this knowledge before, complete and alive in my consciousness. And I didn't have to wait until my thirties to become "more hardened" at the cost of such infamous ordeals ... since so many others were able to resolve this crucial question so much more quickly and positively. That's what's hard. That's what's behind this dissatisfaction with myself that often, very logically, throws me into despair.

This struggle between two worlds being waged within me and within many others like me—will it last forever, to mortify us throughout our entire existence? Or is there some hope that it will end favorably? It seems as though it's inevitable, like a natural phenomenon that occurs in people whose lives have unfolded in circumstances I have known, a phenomenon that most likely will not fail to manifest itself in us again in the future, on the threshold of a new life, like it does in the world described by P. Romanov, Gorki, Gladkov.* These external signs of private battles and moral suffering that destroy and consume. And struggle—the only way of life capable of putting an end to these unhealthy thoughts in an evolving man ... struggle, nothing but struggle.

---

* Fyodor Vasilievich Gladkov (1883–1958): Soviet novelist whose works exalt the industrialization of the USSR and the transformation of social relations. His most well-known work in *Cement*, 1925. (S. H.)

I'm not writing all this to justify myself. There is no justification for faults that we are the first to become fully conscious of, any more so than for shortcomings that we are the first to condemn.

B. B. | August 24, 1944

I am overcome by extreme fatigue and total disinterest. What can I add? A world that is falling apart ... A new world, a saner one, will come along and replace it. I shudder with joy at the thought of a new life, one where clarity and truth will triumph. So many things will finally be explained and discovered, in books, in activity, in life.... And everything will be infinitely simpler, fairer, clearer, so there will be no room for this sort of dilemma.

B. B. | August 26, 1944

There is one thing that baffles me completely. It's to see that men are so much weaker, so much less resilient than women. Physically and often morally, too. They don't know how to get hold of themselves and often display such a lack of courage it's pitiful. Their hunger shows on their faces and in their gestures in a way that's alarmingly different from women.

Many of them either don't know how to discipline their stomachs or else they don't want to or are organically incapable of it. The same goes for thirst, fatigue, their physical reactions to any fundamental deprivation. They lack the strength to adapt, to keep pace.

There are some who have such a miserable demeanor that their misery is much more painful for those who look at them. And there are some whose lack of discipline goes so far as to border on meanness, on overt greediness, on total disloyalty toward their fellow internees in this dire suffering and ordeal that we all share.

Is the whole male sex like this? That's just not possible.... What about those men who are strong in the face of adversity, in the midst of the struggle, who know how to suffer and remain silent with dignity, how to calm and discipline their instincts because they are guided by more humane and lofty impulses than their stomachs or other purely physical needs? This goes without saying: the spectacle before me is nothing other than the natural extension of its protagonists' pasts. In the majority of cases, it is merely a question of their bodies having been used to satisfy their basest instincts without limits, spoiling and fattening up their stomachs for so long a period of time.

For too long, personal pleasures and convenience have been at the center of these people's lives, to the point where privations become unheard-of and tragic things, and self-denial is unthinkable. As for self-discipline, it is an unpleasant novelty that they cannot grasp and that they only accept as necessary for other people. Raising the consciousness of such elements is difficult work, very difficult, nearly impossible; from this perspective they are irresponsible creatures. And this leads to another, much more troubling result: few, very few are those who know how to preserve their dignity before the enemy without cowardice.

B. B. | August 28, 1944

I'm in charge of taking care of the children. There are 110 of them in our barracks, all different ages, from three-year-old infants to fourteen- and fifteen-year-old boys and girls. It's not easy to work without books. I'm forced to write by hand on dozens and dozens of little scraps of paper, filling them with varied content, for the littlest ones who have hardly begun to read and write as well as for the most advanced children. As for paper and pencils, the children manage to acquire them in various ways, by selling their bread rations or engaging in all kinds of transactions, or even stealing them from each other.

Since we have no books, we often have to resort to oral lessons exclusively, which demands particularly sharp attention from the students. On top of that, our lessons are often interrupted, either by *Appell* or by air raid warnings or by inspections—those visits by officials that remind us of ourselves when we used to go to the zoo long ago. Each time there are circumstances beyond our control that disrupt our school work. Or else it's all the chaos and noise right near our "classroom," times when they're hunting for workers, when people are arguing, the commotion when the distribution of soup begins, etc.

The children are unleashed, wild, famished. They feel that their existence has taken an unusual and abnormal turn and they react brutally and instinctively. Bad habits catch on quickly among children in calamitous times and in an overall atmosphere of distrust and fear. A small minority of them shows a keen interest in studying; the others couldn't care less. They are not ignorant of the fact that the Germans have forbidden any true teaching in the camp and that serious study must be undertaken in secret. So they escape from it with impunity.

But it's out of the question to lecture them about it; that would even be ludicrous. All moral lectures have absolutely no effect. The adults get impatient; the children's mischief gets on their nerves. So the adults are sometimes quick to treat the children as "criminals" or "punks." They demand the children be punished in the most severe ways, by making an example of them, taking away their bread rations or whipping them. If for no other reason than to restore some calm! And when they run up against my opposition to such things, they vent their anger against … "such a school and such an education." As if there really could be any education, and as if you could ask children to be nice and polite in a disastrous human environment where all nerves are on edge, where the adults fight among themselves, insult each other, steal from each other, beat each other up without shame or discretion, where everything is warped and corrupted.

The men have forgotten that leading by example is by far more important and effective than any lecture, advice, or punishment. Besides, even in normal or quasi-normal circumstances, didn't teaching and school leave much to be desired in our Slavic homeland? So many things that were absurd, out of step, and poorly adapted to the needs of the people and the times! How often did our work at school seem senseless and useless because of the reactionary nature of the curriculum! We managed with great difficulty to change some aspects of it here and there.... The base remained the same. It's even more absurd to aspire to an ideal education here, in a concentration camp.

Nevertheless, we do what we can, and the children's fundamentally good nature often wins out, and we witness surprising results. Yes, indeed, children have such energy that they can often muster much more than we think them capable of.

Therefore, it's ludicrous to rail against the children for the difficulties they cause when they are the least responsible for them. It's not through beatings and coercion that you extirpate the root causes of difficulties when those root causes are so deeply entrenched that they must be eradicated once and for all. You don't get rid of evil by attacking its effects, but rather by attacking its cause, by pulling it out by the root.

That's why I get overcome with impatience waiting for the new era that will help us to cure this ill by attacking it at its root. It's with immense joy that I imagine the possibilities that will open up to me in my teaching as well. And if my efforts are successful—what happiness! Will I be successful or not? Or will time have passed me by? Always the same doubts, always the same anguish. Because a large part of our being belongs, alas, to this sick and dying world of today—as well as to its past. To hell with it! It's this camp that's depressing me and making me see everything in dark colors....

B. B. | August 29, 1944

Without books, we are ill. I feel beaten down at the core of my being. So many lost hours, so many vanished, inaccessible riches ... What a miserable, sterile existence.... atrophied minds. I spend a lot of time thinking; I'm learning a lot in the midst of this misery; I'm learning how to understand many things in life that escaped me before. But I think about life with regret, *real* life, the life of free human beings, about so much knowledge not acquired over the past several years, and, right here, about so many gaps in knowledge.

There's a kind of pervasive distrust that reigns in the camp and in our barracks. Complete lack of interest in anyone else's fate, lack of solidarity and cordiality. So that you can hardly imagine having any sort of exchange of ideas, about books, any intellectual or even human contact.

B. B. | August 30, 1944

For over a month now everyone has been waiting for an extraordinary event to change our situation directly. The reason: from time to time we get fantastic news about the situation at the front, in the occupied countries, and even in Germany. According to rumors that have been more or less verified, France is almost entirely liberated, Romania is in revolt, the Russians are advancing on Hungary.

We even get reports about headlines in the German newspapers. Titles like "Michael the Romanian's Treason Surpasses Emmanuel the Italian's Treachery" or "All of Germany's Allies, Cowardly, Abandon Her," etc.* And no matter how unrealistic this news seems to us, we are no less excited by it. There are some optimists among us who predict dates and count the days. Like it or not, everyone is caught up in a sort of psychosis anticipating the end. We feel it is near.

And yet, the camp regime has gotten worse and more rigid. This exasperates the internees. Shame and servitude seem even heavier when the end is imminent.

The men working outside are brutally tortured. The German brutes persist in using their favorite method: ferocious blows, rude and hysterical insults. They force the workers to assume the most humiliating positions, running on their knees, dragging carts while they run. All the while, they track them like thieves or, to vary their perverse pleasure, they start a dizzying bicycle race and force the workers to follow them on foot. If one miserable soul, exhausted—and there's always more than one, of course—isn't as zealous as they require, the German "heroes" rush to show their power and their bravery by punishing the

---

* On July 25, 1943, the Italian king Victor Emmanuel III removed Mussolini from office and ordered his arrest. When, in September of the same year, the German invasion took place, he placed himself under the protection of the Allies. Michael I, king of Romania (from 1927 to 1930 and from 1940 to 1947), deposed the dictator Antonescu, an ally of the Nazis, in August 1944, as Soviet troops entered Romania. He abdicated in December 1947. (S. H.)

"guilty parties," taking away their bread ration or putting them in the brig.*

They do all this, of course, while continuously hurling the most outrageous insults at their victims, to the point where you wonder if these people are even capable of speaking calmly and behaving like men even in their private lives.

As for despising and humiliating the Jews, the Nazis are relentless, even though they themselves certainly must know that their end is near. They take advantage of every chance they can to show their contempt for the Jews. The *Appell*—that daily requirement that all internees gather in the courtyard, the *Appellplatz*, and stand at attention in rows so they can be counted by fives—this roll call provides a thousand and one pretexts for them to outwardly express their hatred of Jews.

The regular *Appell* now lasts at least two to three hours longer than it used to; and almost every other day there's some excuse for it to last five or six hours or even the entire day, regardless of weather. But in addition to these regular *Appelle*, there are also times when a sudden order forces us to gather outside (*antreten*) at any time of day, to hear some announcement or another.

Then two or three officers show up and inspect our ranks, and woe to he who moves or disturbs the "order." The scene is unbearable. Especially seeing old men and women, from the south, for example, shivering with cold and fright in front of some pale-faced Prussian criminal. An entire human existence, modest and

---

* Basement cell where the SS jailed "punished" deportees. (S. H.)

honest, filled with years of hard work and a traditional respect for others ... and suddenly they're reduced to standing stiffly at attention in front of these scoundrels who spit demented rage in your face, trample your soul and your dignity.

Or else it's the children who know no joy. Fear, nothing but fear ... these poor little mortified creatures, standing for hours on end, their bodies filled with terror, their gaze fixed, awaiting whatever might happen. They bury their heads in an old rag, press up against the adults, seeking shelter from the cold and the fear. Only their eyes remain wide open, alarmed, like those of a hunted animal.

And the tyrannical German officers observe all this with disdain, demanding "Silence!" A deathly silence does indeed reign in every soul. The officers announce that such and such internee is being sent to the brig, another one transferred to a more rigorous camp, for having stolen some potatoes from the kitchen or a pair of shoes from a depot. Then they display the "criminals," parade them in front of us in the center of the courtyard.

It's like the circus: the "criminals" in the middle, their modest luggage on their backs, surrounded by rows of us, thousands and thousands of human shadows. They stand at attention under a torrent of abuse, awaiting the end of this "ceremony" before their departure.

As for the spectators, they're supposed to learn the lesson well: if they dare imitate the "thieves," they can expect the same consequences or worse. If, on the other hand, your work is satisfactory and you prove to be zealous, enthusiastic, and willing, if you do nothing but run around, obediently, always repeating "*Ja-*

wohl, Herr Oberscharführer," "*jawohl hier*" and "*jawohl her,*"* and if you know to click your heels at all times—and there are always those who do, unfortunately—then you get a bonus, guaranteed: an extra ration of turnip soup or something at any rate. In a word, this is an ideal institute for teaching "respect," where starving creatures are crammed together—a school for forced labor, a correctional facility for miserable, undisciplined, grownup children whose souls were crushed beforehand.

B. B. | August 31, 1944

The JPA,** a mock news agency operated by internees, reports that the Germans are getting ready to evacuate our camp because they need it for military purposes (Bergen-Belsen, located between Hanover, Hamburg, and Bremen in the Celle district; the closest large city is Luneburg). Apparently we will be transferred elsewhere. In the meantime, endless transports of new deportees pour in day and night. Our numbers are increasing and the misery grows endlessly. So are they evacuating or not? Uncertainty reigns because we are caught in their clutches.

There's no *Appell* today. Something must be going on—the arrival or departure of another convoy in the next block (where the criminals and politicals are detained)? Or was there a sudden

---

* " Yes, sir, Oberscharführer," "Yes, sir" here and "Yes, sir" there. (S. H.)
** "Jüdishe Presseagentur" i.e. "Jewish Press Agency." The "Jewish Press Agency" was camp slang among the deportees in Bergen-Belsen for rumors that circulated within the camp. (S. H.)

change in the camp's command? Who knows? The important thing is that there was no *Appell* today, which means that there will surely be one this afternoon or tomorrow, and that it will last twice as long.

B. B. | September 1, 1944

Sure enough, the *Appell* lasted twice as long as usual, allegedly because of a child who didn't show up on time or some such thing. Besides, they leave us standing and waiting for hours on end so frequently that we don't even try to find out the fallacious reason any more.

It's an autumn day. A continuous light rain is falling, a very damp drizzle, along with a powerful wind that reminds me of a stronger, more violent version of our *kochava*.* This morning at roll call we were frozen to the bone.

We spent the whole day replacing our two-level bunk beds with three-level bunks. We only finished about a third of our barracks, which means we've got at least two or three more days of work to do. They've piled us into these three-tier bunks claiming that it will open up some space for a table and make room for people to move around more freely. But it has done nothing of the sort, especially when you consider that we already lacked beds for some fourteen- to sixteen-year-olds.

The end result is that we are even more crowded than before, since each one of us now has a more cramped space for sleeping

---

* A stormy winter wind that blows mostly in Serbia. (S. H.)

and less air to breathe, and we haven't benefited from any "room to move" at all. It is impossible to sit or to move on these three-tier beds. We have just enough room to slip into a hole, provided you curl yourself up tightly before taking your place to sleep and you don't move too much.

The foot traffic between these new bunks is more intense, of course. Being so jammed is enough to drive you crazy. Screams, noise, arguments, moans, infernal turmoil to no end. Endless comings and goings with straw mattresses, bowls of soup, the pathetic nourishment we lug around and devoutly store under reeking rags ... endless comings and goings with boards, pitiful rags, and still-damp laundry. Comings and goings, cries of despair, children's sobs, dust, straw everywhere, the stench, the filth, excrement....

Quarrels are inevitable, especially among the women, either when the beds are being made or when the laundry is being done. Each woman feels uniquely threatened or mocked, a victim of a unique injustice, without realizing that her neighbors are no less miserable. We are all slaves here, and it's on purpose that they've piled us on top of each other, with barely any room to breathe. It's on purpose that they let us insult each other, bicker and argue, to make our existence unbearable, to reduce us to animals, to be better able to mock us, humiliate us, torture us ... the beasts. The suffering is even more dreadful when they cut off our water without warning.

I'm standing near the bed, observing all this, reflecting. People bump into me. People push me. I'm surrounded by filth and screaming. I really don't know where to position myself, where to put myself so as not to bother anyone or myself. I don't know what to do with my body.

The Dutch Jews deported here celebrated their beloved queen's birthday yesterday. They even put on a play. For the children. How can they think of such things? You can't believe your eyes when you see them all dressed up in their Sunday best; the Germans didn't take everything from them as they did us when they were deported here. What makes the Germans decide to act a certain way at certain times?—who will ever know? Nevertheless, our Dutch walk around all spick-and-span! Two young men catch your attention in particular, with their white collars and their ties.... Yes indeed, the queen's birthday is very moving, very moving indeed.

B. B. | September 4, 1944

Our barracks is an insane asylum. Rare are those who know how to control themselves. The slightest incident gives rise to violent quarrels, insults, threats. Everyone has become extremely touchy, always ready to lose their temper and see others as their personal enemy. Distrust, suspicion, and ill will have entered every heart; it makes you shudder.

What a disaster, what a disaster ... these miserable faces on which you can read terror, hunger, primal fear. Especially during the distribution of soup. Each person gets enough to fill two-thirds of a bowl.... They dig down deep into the pot with a large spoon. Such expressions, such a zoological crowd, such tears in the eyes of those who fear that they won't get their share. Panic in the face of uncertainty. Is the pot full enough or only half full?

During this whole time, during this desperate struggle around a spoonful of rutagaba boiled in water, among these screams, these emotions, in the midst of this multitude, in the narrow spaces between beds, the coming and going continues. Bedpans are dragged from one end to the other, depending on whether they are full or empty. And we are never done with these nighttime pans because of the children and the sick....

In this chaos of soup, filth, excrement, brooms, dust, in the midst of the children's screaming and crying, the "merchants," insolent and tiresome, circulate indefatigably, miserable, as miserable as their clients. They exchange rags for bread, bread for cigarettes, and vice versa. These strange dealings are accompanied by long discussions and negotiations without end.

Unbounded misery, shamelessly displayed, foul and shrill. This is exactly what the Nazis wanted, exactly this! To vilify us to this unspeakable degree, to humiliate us to the point of insanity, to kill in us the very memory of having once been human beings.

B. B. | September 6, 1944

They're rounding up laborers again. They violently push the men out of the barracks, punching them, kicking them, beating them with clubs. Everybody out! *Raus!* Men, women, old, young, sick, healthy, no matter. *Antreten!* Lined up in rows, five by five. They count us like we're livestock, or worse, because no one ever thought to pour so much hatred and outrage, so many insults, onto animals.... And so it is that they drag away the new work crew, yelling "*Marsch!*" and "*Los!*" It's repugnant. Is there any equal in the world to the Nazi beast when it comes to rudeness, infamy, the art of physically and morally destroying men? Debauched!

Not far from here, about five to seven hundred meters away, you can clearly see an isolated little camp enclosed by barbed wire. About a hundred Hungarian Jews are interned there. But don't come near! We hear that these people receive packages of food from abroad. The Germans tell us it's a *Sonderlager* (special camp). "Jews?" we ask. "Yes." "Then why is it a *Sonderlager?*" we insist. *"Weil die haben spezielle Papiere."* (Because they have special papers.*) That's the answer. Bizarre.

---

* Hanna Lévy-Hass' diary contains several passages in German that she has either translated in footnotes or in the body of her diary. While her written German in these passages in mostly accurate, the presence of some minor inaccuracies almost certainly reflects the genuine experience of camp inmates who, as she notes early on, spoke over twenty-five languages and who had to adjust to receiving and obeying orders given in a language that they may not have known. Some of her passages in German suggest the possibility that these words and phrases were learned aurally, so their transcription corresponds to what a camp inmate might remember having heard, rather than to strict grammatically correct German usage. (S. H.)

2

B. B. | September 8, 1944

I would so like not to think, not to see all this, but I can't help it. Indifferent and detached from everything around me as I felt just a few weeks ago, today I fully realize that my life is irrevocably tied to the life of this camp and that we are all, like it or not, united by the same fate and in the same misery.

I could write and write, hundreds and thousands of pages— and I would never manage to exhaust all the misery, to bring out all the bitter details of our existence. Especially if I were to begin to enumerate all the cases of personal disaster, the tragedy of former lives, the great individual sufferings that came before this, the collective misery, the total continuity of the curse … it would be endless! Because the volume of man's pain is immense; it's impossible to measure this ocean of suffering; the abyss of the human soul under terror and torture is unfathomable. To try to describe all this—a useless endeavor. It far exceeds my capabilities.

More than once, at certain moments of our enslavement, confronted by the desperate torment of the masses, I have thought of Dante's *Inferno*. And not for the pleasure of literary reminiscence. It's just that the images of Hell that we are used to imagining were the only feelings that my mind was able to conjure up. It wasn't in my power to evoke any other memory; that was the only idea still alive in my mind.

The horror that surrounds us is so great that the brain becomes paralyzed and completely incapable of reacting to anything that doesn't stem directly from the nightmare we are presently living through and that is constantly before our eyes.

That's why I am incapable at this time of recalling anything from the past except what we lived through most recently: the trip they made us take to get here. What an ordeal! Two weeks in cattle cars. Piled up, forty to sixty per car, men, women, the elderly, children. Hermetically sealed, with no air, no light, no water, no food … we were suffocating in a tiny space saturated with filth, fumes, sweat, stench … ravaged by thirst and lack of space.

Only twice during those two weeks did they give us a little bit of water and some tins of food. We were "lucky" when we crossed Czechoslovakia. The Czech Red Cross treated us to nice warm soup. We almost fainted with delight.… Then they gave us some water. You had to see the expressions carved on the Czechs' faces as they watched us fighting over every drop. Who knows what they read in our eyes and on our faces!

And the distressing trip continued. The Germans refused to open the train cars for even the most basic needs. Only three times during the whole trip were we able to get out and relieve ourselves. But it was so humiliating and shameful that I still blush. In the midst of a splendid countryside, in a large, open field ... and us, so ill at ease. The Nazi soldiers kept close to us, shamelessly watching us go and even calling on us to hurry up.... standing so close to us, pointing their rifles, supervising us.

All this accompanied by insults, jeers, savage and sadistic screaming aimed at those who, sick, mortified, pitiful, exhausted by hunger and constant thirst, humiliated in the extreme, didn't manage to finish what they were doing. I didn't notice one single time, not once, the slightest indication of a human reaction, the slightest hint of difficulty or discomfort in these soldiers who were under orders to behave as they did. Nothing! Their faces didn't reveal anything human....

At night, under a torrent of gunfire and machine-gun fire, the train crossed regions under attack by partisans or airplanes. There was one air raid siren after another. The Germans would get out of the train and take shelter wherever they could while we remained, piled up in the box cars, very visible on the tracks, panic-stricken.

Inside, in the dark, the children screamed at the top of their voices, the women wailed, the men argued over space. Exasperated, driven mad, people didn't cease quarrelling and telling each other to go to hell. We had an insane desire to stretch out and we couldn't. In these deplorable conditions, there was no question of falling asleep, since even breathing was impossible.... It was Hell.

And when we finally arrived at our destination, not having the slightest idea where we were, and when we climbed out of our holes ... it was like wild animals emerging from the shadows of death. Then the sad procession began: faded and yellow like the ground, starved, exhausted, pale, fever in our eyes, we dragged ourselves like worn-out rags along an endless road that led to the Bergen-Belsen camp, dirty and sweating under the weight of what remained of our miserable possessions.

Frightening human shadows—mute, slow—moved along an unknown road. The inhabitants of the villages—women in coquettish summer dresses, passersby on bikes or on foot, all fresh and properly dressed and groomed, with the calm that comes from a normal life engraved on their faces—would stop for a moment and look at us with curiosity ... and with absolute indifference! Without ever letting go their rifles, numerous soldiers walked along the columns we formed, doling out their club blows to whoever dared turn around or fall slightly behind.

It's at this moment that the wounded soul began to take on the outrage and shame that, later, would accumulate, forming a mountain of torture.

B. B. | September 17, 1944

Misery and pain suffocate me. And *hatred*. Happy are those who don't suffer in hatred. Personally, I can't help it. I constantly get tears in my eyes, tears of rage and shame. How bitter is the poisoned soul.... Tears of rage and shame suffocate me. The cry of unjustly and brutally suppressed feelings weakens me. It's so hard, so hard, I am so afraid of feeling it all over again. Sobs of injustice and misery in the world. Sobs of injustice and misery within me tear me apart.

B. B. | September 25, 1944

They are building new barracks. For whom? No one knows. But we can guess. There is renewed talk of large convoys being sent to the camp. Rapidly, feverishly, in almost every bit of space between the old barracks, construction is going on. Everyone has been put to work. The hunt for laborers, roundups, curses, thrashings ... all of it gets repeated, again and again, endlessly.

In response to sabotage, the Germans are reducing our bread rations every day. The men are worn out. Undernourishment, the shortage of cigarettes for the smokers, and forced labor have pushed them to the brink. I see some men picking up cigarette butts that the Germans have thrown away in the courtyard or going to the trash cans near the kitchen to salvage some smelly remnants of food.

Inside the barracks, the situation is hardly any better. Famine is devouring everyone. A nameless epidemic is invading the camp, affecting the women and children especially. It takes the form of a high fever that lasts two or three weeks, loss of consciousness, complete exhaustion, and the loss of all appetite. There is no perceptible pain. The doctors call it "camp fever" or "para-typhoid fever"—what do I know—and claim that the symptoms don't allow for a precise diagnosis. One out of every two beds is almost always occupied by someone who's sick.

Then there are the abscesses and open wounds, due to the vermin or undernourishment; permanently oozing sores, boils, sprains, abnormal swelling (edemas), cramps, various infections … this has all become commonplace for us.

Medication is rare or nonexistent. We understand that it's out of the question to give medical assistance to the sick, true medical assistance; the point is to let them either get well or die, as chance would have it, depending on their own body's strength.

With all this, the faucets remain dry for no good reason three-quarters of the time. The pretext used this time is that the central baths need water for the showers … and yet, it's been two and a half months since we've been given access to the baths.

It's plain to see that these interruptions in water supply strangely coincide with the spread of epidemics and the increasing need for water to guard against so much misery. We are deprived of the most essential thing necessary to maintain any cleanliness or minimal hygiene: water.

Autumn is approaching, indifferently. The bleak perspective of a deadly winter makes us shudder with dread. In the meantime, rain and mud. All day long we move about surrounded by the noise of construction—the clatter of boards and the banging of hammers. They are building new barracks.

B. B. | October 11, 1944

Everything is relative, of course. Each one of us will speak of this camp of horror in his own way. There will be many of these "truths!" Different, relative, variable truths. Everything depends on the subjective point of view of your particular situation, where you position yourself in your observations and the individual prism through which you watch the whole scene…. I have recently learned some rather curious things: six to eight hundred of the seven thousand people who occupy our block are employed in various internal and external work. Thanks to their opportunistic attitude open to compromises of conscience—with the help of their ingratiating personality—these people are placed in exceptionally favorable situations and receive amazing quantities of the best supplies and clothing; in other words, they get or have the possibility of obtaining everything they need—and then some. Which means that, for some time now, they have completely forgotten the suffering of others. Numbed by the unprecedented abundance in which they live, they don't realize that others are literally dying of hunger and would like a bite of bread, at least…. Some among them have lost all moral compass, all scruples. Happy to be alive and to eat, they can't find enough good things to say about this or that German. They are perfectly comfortable developing theories that explain that the Germans are only rude and brutal because many of us are inept, clumsy, apathetic, and don't know how to work. "It gets on the Germans' nerves, you know, you have to understand, it's revolting for them, with reason. Aside from that, the Germans are very well mannered, very polite toward honest, intelligent workers; they're even very friendly toward them…"

Pitiful reasoning, but frequent all the same, precisely in those among us who are considered "serious," "solid," "intellectuals." R. the engineer is particularly good at this sort of logic. All the same … but there's no point in arguing, he's not an ignorant person. He knows very well that the Germans can only be polite and relatively human toward precisely those who show them sympathy and agreement, toward precisely those who are ready and determined, in words and in deeds, to side openly with the Nazis, their entire program and their methods. And that it's highly doubtful that these Nazis seriously trust them, since they received their training at the school of chauvinistic lunacy and absolute disdain for others.… The wretch knows very well that the Germans' behavior is far from "polite" and "well mannered" toward he who remains cold, passive, reserved toward them, showing clearly that he is conscious of his status as a deportee, a slave—and the Germans' status as his enemy, nothing but his enemy. Obviously, the Germans don't treat such a man gently.

Still, these "lucky ones," having succeeded in getting placed in favorable conditions, pursue the classic reasoning of cowards and opportunists: "The essential thing, right now, is to save your own skin, to get out alive, come what may.... And besides, *we* know what we think." In the meantime they, their family, and their friends benefit greatly from their privilege. You can find these "lucky ones" who sometimes don't hesitate to declare themselves overtly germanophile, everywhere—in the food and clothing storehouses, at internal and external work sites, at the train station, in the kitchens of the SS and other military personnel, in the kitchens of Camps 1 and 2.

They try very hard to convince us that the well-being that they enjoy does not in any way harm the other internees or their basic interests as internees. They claim that their material comforts are not based on the dispossession of those in the camp who are starving, those who don't enjoy the Nazis' favors—that's the way it is; it's luck, you know!

But the fact is that they hardly care about what goes on inside the blocks—inside the blocks infested with vermin, famine, fever, death, decay—not to mention the moral anguish. They close their eyes, cover their ears, they don't want to see, they don't want to hear—they haven't the slightest clue about all this. And they're the ones who say it, moreover. Most of them live in separate barracks where they are housed relatively well, where they have created a world of their own. It should come as no surprise to hear bursts of laughter and singing coming from their barracks, to see everyone in a good mood. They return from work well-nourished and in good disposition. They carefully groom themselves, organize dinner parties, feasts, cocktails, and concerts. Their wives have first-rate linens, their beds are perfumed. They have a knack for décor. They tell jokes and make love.

And it goes without saying that they don't neglect the camp administrators. They share their wealth with the barracks' chiefs, those who do not work but nonetheless have contact, even if seemingly official, with the Germans, those who live under a special system, less harsh.... So this group laughs, flirts, and it's so innocent: live and let live! Who knows what the future holds, etc.

These people will have very different things to tell about the camp, about the Germans, about everything that went on. There will even be some who will have fond memories of this place, memories of pleasant days, of the Germans' "kindness," of a vague feeling of happiness, of how "lucky" they will have been.... Everything is relative, of course, there's no denying it.

B. B. | October 17, 1944

Something just happened in the next camp. Polish women are interned there, but it is not clear whether they are Jewish or political deportees. All we know is that they are treated worse than we are. Some of them live under special surveillance. They must have rebelled today, decided to do something and protested. The shock-waves came our way; an order was suddenly given to suspend all movement, the workers returned before the end of the workday, in the kitchens, they had to turn off the fire and the personnel evacuated the area. The doors separating our blocks from the rest of the camp were closed. Total silence and panic.

We will never really know how things ended over there where the rebels are. But it's clear that the Germans have "restored order" as they always do, committing further crimes. The crematoria are running nonstop, overtly, for all to see.

Behind the complex of blocks where we are all piled up, there are still more barracks, in all directions, as far as the eye can see, where the political prisoners and criminals they call *Häftlinge* are interned; there's a crowd of fifty to sixty thousand people, women and children who've been imprisoned for any excuse imaginable.

And every day the processions of new arrivals drag themselves along on the roads between the blocks, an entire army of miserable souls being led to forced labor and already they are exhausted, famished, tormented. Several hundred of these new arrivals have been placed near us, a hundred steps away, on the other side of the barbed wire. We don't dare approach them, but we would like to…. The Germans shoot, for fear that we might tell each other those horrible truths we hold—or they hold. They are afraid, the Germans, they are truly frightened of us—this human livestock that they have reduced to an inert and disconsolate mass. The proof of this lies in what happened today.

B. B. | October 18, 1944

Among the dead that were removed from the hospital today—the hospital, a barracks like any other—three had belonged to our barracks. And among these three was a young, fourteen-year-old girl. Before the war, she was a strong, beautiful child. In prison at Podgorica,* she already had a flu that quickly turned into tuberculosis. When we arrived here four months ago, she was already near the end. She was fading slowly every day, before our eyes. In the past couple of days her suffering reached its height. She was no longer able to move in the slightest. Her mother isn't making a scene; she's calm, resigned. She still has two daughters, younger, both very pretty, but they are also becoming shadows due to their constant hunger. These young bodies need to eat, to grow, or else they are like young plants that dry up.

Their father disappeared two years ago when the Ustasa** took him. And now they are losing their older sister. This morning we saw her skinny young body, so skinny. A corpse, a few lifeless bones, wrapped in one of the camp's light gray blankets. She was laid on two narrow old planks in a kind of laboratory. Right above her lifeless head were some dirty test tubes on a shelf, a modest, uncovered window looking out on the gray barbed-wire barrier and beyond, the lines of dull, gray barracks ... and then

---

* The second-largest city in Montenegro after the capital. (S. H.)
** Armed Croatian collaborationist militia. (S. H.)

the void, a cold, dreary, foggy, empty space, the rainy line of the pale, damp, mouse-colored Nordic horizon....

By way of a funeral, we were permitted to walk all of thirty paces to accompany the miserable wooden coffin to the central gate. There, the barbed wire fence was opened to let the corpse through, alone, on a cart; the little one went out toward "freedom." She died at one o'clock, in the middle of the night. No doubt by now she has already been quickly consumed by the flames.

B. B. | October 20, 1944

This morning a small, elderly woman died in the barracks, very near to my bed. The family cried a little and then got rid of the body. An ended life, quickly forgotten. We are dazed. Each one of us is buried in their own misery. And yet, the color of this shared, collective misery gets clearer and clearer.

There are cases of brain sicknesses now, a sort of cerebral in-flammation. The camp epidemic is everywhere. The little children suffer from some peculiar illnesses. An adorable little four-year-old girl has been in bed for five weeks with excessively high fever. She's covered with boils. When her mother sits her up on the bed, her head droops over her shoulder; she doesn't have the strength to hold it upright. She watches her surroundings with a knowing, intelligent, and resigned look. Her marvelous, big eyes are the only part of her emaciated face that still has life. And once her little body is undressed, it is nothing but a skeleton ... a skeleton that still breathes, lives, suffers, and falls silent. Without tears, without screams. Besides, she doesn't have the strength for that. This morning, they lanced her boils—it's horrible, so much pus. She sobbed just a little bit—and the rest of the time she was silent, immobile. A little martyr, a sad symbol of misfortune and resignation.

B. B. | October 22, 1944

Much commotion reigned in our barracks last week. As I have already observed, distrust and intolerance are common to everyone. Let's add to this the fact that relationships imposed between the internees most often take unpleasant and unfortunate forms: corruption, deceit, trickery. Those who enjoy a certain "ability" or "skill" or who possess a "practical mind" or who keep close to the Germans (which is all one and the same, really), all those who have adopted an attitude devoid of scruples and principles toward men and the world in general, these people manage to benefit from any situation at the expense of other detainees.

This is how things work, beginning at the top, with the *Judenälteste*, ("Jewish elder") who is our "representative" to the Germans, on down through the various members of his entourage in charge of different "elite" operations in the camp, to the leaders of each barracks surrounded by their aides and accomplices. This creates very distinct castes in camp life: there are those who suffer, die of hunger and illness, work hard, are beaten and mistreated, without pity and at every turn—while the others live in relative tranquility, well-nourished, taken care of, protected at the expense of the rest of the detainees. Little by little they lose all consciousness of our shared fate and all sense of solidarity.

In the beginning, I just observed all this and, feeling power-less, did not intervene, but stayed "neutral." But inside our bar-racks, where the general state of things is faithfully reflected, the organized and systematic thefts, abuse, deceit, corruption, and all that flows from this have reached untenable proportions. The way in which these plots are carried out is so rude, so repugnant, and so cowardly that you are overcome by complete disgust. Everyone knows that large quantities of the food allocated for the barracks, and in particular a good portion of the daily soup, disappears mysteriously and methodically. A feverish, shameless market has erupted in our barracks. An entire system of orders, of supply and demand among those busy exchanging what the rest of us con-sider fantastic merchandise (silk stockings, rings, jewelry, furs, boots, entrancing cosmetics, etc.) ... and alongside all this, bowls filled with aromatic soup, all kinds of appetizing foodstuffs that make us dizzy, circulate openly and constantly, carving out a path for themselves among the starving, bewildered, dying masses. In-dignation, jealousy, suspicion, doubt, in each and toward each, founded or unfounded ... the air is completely poisoned.

Our barracks is divided into two sections, one for the men and the other one for the women and children. The separation is not that strict, but even so.... Among the men, distrust appears sporadically, through outbursts of personal hatred, swearing, threats: "Thief, you'll see ..." "Son of a ..." etc. As for the thief, he either reacts or doesn't, depending on the situation, or else quite frequently he ends up corrupting his adversary. To rein in all this infamy, we would naturally need a shared, collective spirit of action, of unity, of agreement and understanding. But that's not our strong point.

In the women's section, it's the same or nearly so. Sometimes it's even noisier; you witness outbursts of hysteria, lamentation, curses—without anyone getting the slightest notion to do something concrete and effective. Nevertheless, above all because of the children they are responsible for, the women sometimes show more practical and collectivist tendencies. They stubbornly try to find a way out, sometimes demonstrating true courage, and are ready to make sacrifices if necessary. Last Saturday, you could notice a certain agitation accompanied by consultations among some of the women. Then they came to me and pleaded with me to take control of the situation. That's how the battle began Saturday evening and continued throughout the entire week. We won, to everyone's satisfaction. Here's how it all went:

First, after an improvised meeting near my bed and in the name of 120 women in the section, we demanded explanations from Mrs. R., the head of the section, about the distribution of food. She professed her loyalty; we let her know that if she wanted to dissipate any suspicions, all she had to do was to agree to cooperate with the delegates elected to help with distribution and to guarantee the supervision demanded by all the women. Mrs. R., who is also the wife of the barracks chief but who is not very energetic, seeing that her back was against the wall, could only yield to the decision of the majority.

After that we made further demands, requiring that the men's section put an end to the practice of giving an extra dish of soup, taken from our rations, to the soup carriers. Knowing these men, these six to eight vat carriers, freed up from any outside work and whose sole job consisted of carrying eight or ten soup vats a day, returning them empty to the kitchens—we demanded the immediate end of their undeserved privileges. Several considerations supported our demands: hundreds of workers without these advantages who went out daily to do forced labor, who were exposed to the Nazis' indescribable torments for ten or twelve hours a day, and who never received any extra rations, any help from the collective, and who knew that they couldn't even aspire to such things. On the other hand, those famous soup vat carriers, on the pretext of collecting their seemingly meager extra ration, engage in all sorts of wheeling and dealing, thanks especially to this monopoly over the vats. All this in such a way that the others cannot watch over them and see things for what they are.

The women decided not to grant any extra rations or any privilege to the men who carry the soup to the women's section. If they refused to deliver the vats to us "free of charge," we were determined to set up a voluntary service among the women who had more or less conserved some physical strength, in order to ensure steady provisions for our section. The following day, on

Sunday, these two decisions were put into effect, which aroused a lively interest among all the inhabitants of the barracks.

Everything was working for the better, until the barracks chief, the *Barackenleiter*, the women's section's director's husband (and former representative of the Swedish match trust in Yugoslavia), sensed that this action organized by women didn't sit well with him at all. Therefore, appealing to others and supported by his first assistant in particular (an extremely crafty man with a dangerously keen if primitive intelligence), he set about creating obstacles for us and putting up all sorts of impediments to the execution of our project. It was clear to everyone that the system chosen by the women did not please the barracks' administrators in the least, since it threatened to convince others of the need for an even wider reorganization of tasks. Our adversaries displayed unbelievable malice and guile. An entire set of refined, well-calculated tactics constructed of both traps and subterfuge. But we did not back down. The women, confident and brave, supported me courageously. Thus we were able to predict and prevent each of the adversary's new maneuvers.

Suddenly, I felt within me an extraordinary strength, a surprising firmness and resolve, with which I was extremely pleased. Nothing could intimidate me. I was not unaware that I was dealing with an adversary who was clearly stronger than me, since the Germans favored him—he held power here, in some ways—and since, precisely because of his position, it wouldn't take much for him to go denounce the whole situation to the German camp commander.

And yet, we held our ground.... The justness of the cause and the mass suffering inspired a noble courage in each fighter. And when the barracks chief and his acolytes realized that we would stand up for ourselves and that we were determined to fight to the end, even if it meant submitting to the "bunker," and that we carried out our task as vat carriers with honor (they forced us to get up very early, before the dawn, in harsh cold weather, claiming that if we didn't our vats would be stolen by people from other blocks, etc.), when they understood that we knew what we wanted—at that moment something happened that completely showed the barracks chief's true colors.

One morning, he appeared abruptly in the women's section and brutally announced in a dictatorial tone (he's far from being a hero; he's a coward who cries when he's hungry) that the "women's reign" (*Wirtschaft*—he was using the German word) was henceforth abolished, that he would not permit any competing action, that he would not tolerate any "soviets" or "republics" in any barracks that was entrusted to him. To which the women retorted that they were determined to continue what they deemed advantageous for the collective and what the collective had already agreed upon, that they didn't need a dictatorship in these already sufficiently severe conditions, that they refused to put up with a double enslavement, and that, if there was a recourse to violence to crush our initiative, the women and children would go on a hunger strike.

For all these reasons—and also influenced and advised by people more capable than he and who feared that this whole affair might expose the corridors where even more complicated and incriminating politics went on—the barracks chief changed his mind, quickly shifted his tone and his tactics, and acquiesced to our demands. That's how we won two officially recognized victories: first, no reward would be doled out to the vat carriers who were expected to perform their task according to principles of equality and solidarity in forced work and suffering. Second, the distribution of food in the women's section would be done equitably, openly, and without secrecy, such that all hundred and twenty women could know at all times where every mouthful went. Any eventual surplus would be shared regularly, in turn, once the regular distribution was complete. To oversee the new distribution system, we chose personnel in charge, drew up lists, developed a numbering system, etc.

This entire episode was of great importance to me. It enriched me with precious experience. I realized that people of dubious character and conscience are not as strong as they would have us believe, and that it's possible to win out over them in an open struggle. I also ascertained that I was still capable of finding my bearings, of choosing the adequate tactic—that my brain was not irrevocably numb, that I emerged easily from torpor and still found enough freshness and strength within me for a just battle.... And that my knowledge of life and of human character types, acquired over these past several years, had borne fruit. I ascertained as well that I had seriously matured and that I was much stronger and surer of myself than previously.

And I learned many details necessary to the struggle, crucial little tactical rules: prudence, patience, the necessity of considering a point in all its aspects before coming to a decision; in negotiations with the adversary, keep your calm, with a resolute, fearless mind; once a decision is made, act on it methodically, according to the prescribed plan, which is also the best way to create obstacles for your adversary and make him back down ... especially when you're dealing with an adversary whose power is only apparent.

And I learned one other thing, which is not negligible: in times of struggle, of action, you always have to reckon with an annoying and persistent obstacle raised by the typical opposition of mean, petty people with no principles, with crude ideas, poor imagination, people incapable not only of undertaking but even of conceiving of something positive, socially oriented, collective; people always ready to disturb others' minds, to sow distrust, to impede the course of things. These are the supreme petty bourgeois types, small-minded, mediocre, pitiable, surly, and refusing to allow or comprehend anything imaginable that doesn't lead to an immediate profit for them; these are those corrupting natures that sometimes groan against corruption, but only out of envy, because they are ready to keep silent as soon as they are allowed to play the game. This moral putrefaction functions as the ideal lubricant for the development of reactionary elements in society....

B. B. | October 23, 1944

Judging by the news that sometimes reaches us here, many of our cities in the distant homeland are already liberated. A violent nostalgia torments us. Back there, people move around freely, each one attending to his business. And clarity has already penetrated people's souls. In the meantime, we are behind barbed wire, reduced to an inhumane existence.

B. B. | October 23, 1944

Every day there's an air raid warning after six-thirty in the evening such that we are left in total darkness all evening and all night. The men return from work in darkness, they have to find their place in the barracks gropingly, and they have to eat their humble meal in the dark as well. The darkness adds to the overall state of agitation, people jostle each other; frightened, crowded, and irritated, the children let out piercing screams, people call out to each other blindly and yell into the shadows from one end of the barracks to the other. All manner of thieves make use of the total darkness. They especially go after the bread, the main currency for trafficking in the camp and the sole substance that prolongs our existence in the slightest.

The struggle for bread, a desperate struggle for the tiniest crumb, the anguish of being deprived or stripped of it by either thieves or the Germans—who amuse themselves at times by letting us go several days without this basic ration—this has become the most immediate, the most emotional concern for each one individually and for all the internees in general. The rations get systematically smaller every week. The daily ration, measured here in centimeters, is today only 3.5 cm. People tremble for this piece as though for gold. They cut it cautiously, devotedly, into slices only one or two millimeters thick. So it's a tragedy when someone swipes your ration or when, for some reason or another—or for no reason—you are punished by being denied one or two rations of bread....

And yet, in spite of all the inconveniences of the darkness, in spite of the mortifying anguish, of the deafening noise, of the risk of getting robbed, we are all content when the air raid warning comes. First, I would say there is a sort of complacent indifference in the face of the possibility of an Allied aerial attack. That's because we calculate logically: surely they're not going to come and drop their bombs on barracks full of deportees ... even though this possibility is not out of the question. And then, it's because at the end of the day these air raid warnings are the only pleasant thing that we experience, the only thing that connects us to the outside world and feeds our hope....

This morning, dawn broke, clear and frozen; the barracks' roofs were covered by a thick layer of ice. In the courtyard, the ponds were frozen. November will be here soon. We still have hope. The course of world events works in our favor—without a doubt.

I regularly take care of the children. I distinctly feel that our "school" has become indispensable and that it's the only way to revive and maintain any freshness in their souls. The vast majority of the children evince a strong desire to study, to make up for lost time; it is with cries of joy and "hooray!" that they welcome my calls to gather together. The most resourceful among them then fight to get a free corner in the barracks where we can have class. They all settle in and I see adorable children's faces around me, on which I read both cheerfulness and concentration.

On days when we are prevented from studying, the students' mood changes visibly; they become bored and indignant at seeing themselves reduced only to a sensation of hunger, at having no human activity. Because it is truly a deplorable thing that children, at an age when their minds and bodies struggle to develop, are reduced to physical and moral vegetation in humiliating conditions of mass servitude that distort and defeat their energy.

That's why I push myself to make them study as often as possible. With the very youngest, it's irresistible: they have become so attached to me that there would be no way to extricate myself from them. As for the older children, they currently study with me, because of Professor K.'s illness and the complete indifference of all the other "pedagogues." The older children's class has a particular flavor to it. They like to discuss various problems of life with me, which allows me to guide them toward ideas I hold dear. That's how it came to be that the other day, I had them read and discuss Verhaeren's poem entitled "Effort" (found here by chance and translated into Serbian). The simplicity of his description of human labor in this poem aroused a lively interest on the part of the students. They began spontaneously to talk about everything they knew about various trades, and I gently pushed them to point out the value of work, the role of workers in society, in the development of the earth's wealth, in production, etc. From there, they went on to ascertain that a tight bond unites the fate of civilized humanity to working-class consciousness and movement. Thanks to the fact that a good part of my students are of working-class origins, from families of farmers and craftsmen from the southern regions of Yugoslavia (Kosovo and Metohija), I was able to concretize the discussion and help the students acquire knowledge based on their own experiences.

I am still in charge of the distribution of food, as it was decided. But more and more I realize that it is difficult and even illusory to expect any serious and lasting success because it all takes place in these horrible conditions where an amorphous and divided human mass struggles. What's more, the guile and treachery of these morally decadent, sinister types who, like predatory animals, insist on wanting only to save their own skin while playing with the lives of hundreds of their fellow men is beyond me. I feel like I can't take it, all alone, confronted with so much depravity and meanness.

B. B. | November 6, 1944

A large transport of women arrived again a few days ago. It held seventeen hundred women of different nationalities, most of them of Jewish origin. They were transferred from Auschwitz. According to rumors, the camp at Auschwitz has already been liquidated, or nearly so. These women who have just arrived are among the rare survivors. There are some who come from our northern regions (Vojvodina or Croatia). They were all recently deported, so we can't find out anything definite about the fate of our loved ones who were sent to Poland in 1941 and 1942. Apparently, there are no living witnesses of the horrible crimes perpetrated in 1941.

Here, the new arrivals are crammed together in tents. They sleep on a thin layer of straw or, more precisely, on the bare, wet ground. They look dreadful, sick, withered, covered with foul and filthy wounds. It's impossible to get near them or talk to them. In the evening, on the pretext of going to the WC, we perceive in the dusk an oppressive noise that rises up like a black tide from the other side of the barbed wire, mixed with children's sobs, with moans, groans, and complaints. There's no way to make out a single word. This baleful hum of a human mass is at once poignant and dreadful.

Every day, the barracks are subject to a severe inspection. By a young SS woman, a "gray mouse," elegant and coquettish in her uniform, spick-and-span; cute shiny boots up to her knees. She intrudes into the barracks, arrogant, noisy, accompanied by a soldier and the Jewish commander of the camp (the *Judenälteste*). The "gray mouse" makes excessive, aggressive gestures, swings her whole body around, and lets out cries of horror, theatrically calculated, on seeing a poorly washed bowl or a poorly made bed. She excels in slapping you in the face at full force, sudden, impetuous, rapid slaps, without ever removing her glove.... And she punishes at least seven or eight internees in each barracks every day by depriving them of bread or soup. Intimidate, quibble, humiliate, for the slightest thing—that's her only goal. These visits have no other meaning. Because fundamentally the Germans do not now nor do they intend to adopt even the slightest serious measures against infection and filth—both of course fatal and without remedy in these vile conditions in which they themselves have forced us to "live" and to die. Their visits and their "inspections" are nothing but formalities. So no one among us is impressed by the loud extravagances and perverted profanities of this creature beyond belief. But what is repulsive is the fact that every morning you are forced to witness these humiliating scenes, to feel this anxiety invade the air, to be confronted by these servile expressions on people's faces.

With the severe cold of the past several days and the forced fast that has systematically sapped our bodies for two months, we all feel extremely weakened. The sensation of hunger is pervasive: your stomach empty, your mind constantly, painfully preoccupied with a mad desire to eat till you're full, endless conversations about all kinds of dishes. If someone is fortunate enough to find or steal a raw turnip ... it's a feast for his whole entourage.

B. B. | November 8, 1944

I would love to feel something pleasant, aesthetic, to awaken nobler, tender feelings, dignified emotions. It's hard. I press my imagination, but nothing comes. Our existence has something cruel, beastly about it. Everything human is reduced to zero. Bonds of friendship remain in place only by force of habit, but intolerance is generally the victor. Memories of beauty are erased; the artistic joys of the past are inconceivable in our current state. The brain is as if paralyzed, the spirit violated.

The moral bruises run so deep that our entire being seems atrophied by them. We have the impression that we're separated from the normal world of the past by a massive, thick wall. Our emotional capacity seems blunt, faded. We no longer even remember our own past. No matter how hard I strive to reconstruct the slightest element of my past life, not a single human memory comes back to me.

We have not died, but we are dead. They've managed to kill in us not only our right to life in the present and for many of us, to be sure, the right to a future life ... but what is most tragic is that they have succeeded, with their sadistic and depraved methods, in killing in us all sense of a human life in our past, all feeling of normal human beings endowed with a normal past, up to even the very consciousness of having existed at one time as human beings worthy of this name.

I turn things over in my mind, I want to ... and I remember absolutely nothing. It's as though it wasn't me. Everything is expunged from my mind. During the first few weeks, we were still somewhat connected to our past lives internally; we still had a taste for dreams, for memories. But the humiliating and degrading life of the camp has so brutally sliced apart our cohesion that any moral effort to distance ourselves in the slightest from the dark reality around us ends up being grotesque—a useless torment. Our soul is as though caught in a crust that nothing can soften or break.

And to think that this is only our fifth month here and that we are in a camp that, if you believe the Germans, is not among the worst.... And yet, what a deadly night!

I will definitely remember everything I have seen, experienced, and learned, everything that human nature has revealed to me. From this moment on it is encrusted in the depths of my soul. And in normal life (but what is in essence normal? All this, this eternalized anguish—or rather what is beyond, before and after?) I will never again be able to forget, I believe, the findings and verdicts arrived at here: I will measure each man against the criteria of today's reality, from the perspective of what he was or could have been in these conditions of ours. To form an opinion of someone, to have a high opinion of him or not, to like him or not, everything will depend first and foremost on knowing what his behavior, his physical, moral and psychological reaction was or might have been during these dark years characterized by great trials—the force of his character, his emotional endurance. I will no longer be able to separate my thoughts from my understanding of war's events; the two will be intimately linked forever in my mind.

B. B. | November 18, 1944

In spite of everything, my work with the children continues. The others—the "adults" and the "competent ones"—instead of helping me, do nothing but create obstacles for me. I cling desperately to every chance, however slight, to gather the children together to foster in them and in me even the slightest mental sharpness, as well as a basic feeling of human dignity.

It was decided in the camp that Saturdays would be devoted to children's entertainment, mostly of a religious nature. In our barracks, we are also taking advantage of Saturdays to provide the children with some amusement, but adapted mostly to the overall mentality of the people here: oral recitations, singing solo or in chorus, small theatrical productions. Given the total lack of books, I collect and write down the material for these performances based on the children's memories and my own and more often than not, we must resort to improvising texts or poetic lines. A whole throng of known tunes have been recovered thanks to the tireless efforts and concentration of all my students—but the words escape us as if they had been sucked into a pit. So we begin to invent lines, to rhyme, to create texts that affect us deeply, to invoke our distant homeland, glorious and heroic....

I carry out this task spontaneously, even instinctively I would say, through an irresistible need in my soul—in the rare moments when I manage to awaken it—and by an irresistible need that I can clearly sense coming from the children's souls. Because they take my lead, they get excited, they want to live, they want to rejoice, it's stronger than them. What heartbreak!

B. B. | November 20, 1944

There is something strange and frightening about a human being's ability to adapt to anything: to humiliation, to degrading hunger, to the lack of vital space, to fetid air, to infection, to washing oneself in a group.... This group washing exceeds everything a normal imagination could possibly conceive: we remain standing, all of us, undressed, in an area that has only gaping holes as windows and doors and that is hammered from all sides by gusts of wind.... We wash, we scrub ourselves with icy water ... and we get used to it—just as we get used to the mounting terror, to the most cynical brutality, to the sirens and the threats, to the mass illnesses, to multifarious, collective, slow but certain death. Man gets used to it, he does. Pinned down, miserable, terrorized ... he gets used to it! He sinks lower and lower. And if he doesn't hang on, he dies. That's his only response. And the rest of us continue to drag on, and to sink also, continually lower and lower. What horror! This death without dying, this prolonged living death....

B. B. | November 22, 1944

Ch. just died unexpectedly. He was a well-built, solid man. At the age of sixty-five, he had retained, even here in the camp, some remnants of his admirable freshness from the past. And then here he was, weighed down by unhappiness, stretched out on his bed for only three days until, with the help of exhaustion and hunger, he passed away.... In three days it was all over.

Yesterday the *Appell* lasted all day and into the night, in the wind and rain. Five people were missing. This morning, they were "found."

For over a month all we've had to eat is one bowl of soup per day. Soup? In a manner of speaking. Rutabagas boiled in water. And such horrible water! But that's it...rutabagas in water. On the ground, in front of and behind the barbed wire. Everywhere. Wherever you turn, wherever you look, there are rutabagas, endless rutabagas. Mountains of rutabagas. rutabagas, rutabagas, rutabagas—in the carts, in front of the doors, in front of the kitchens, in the underground depots—everywhere.

This gray turnip that is normally used to feed animals—we are made to eat, we are made to want it by having been abandoned over and over to the claws of consuming hunger. Oh, such hunger! rutabagas, we'll eat rutabagas all winter long. Unless we die first.... Germany, land of blessings, land of rutabagas, of ersatz, of concentration camps, of slavery and terror.

Allied planes fly over us constantly. The air raid sirens never end. All of Germany is being bombed. The sirens sound two or three times each and every day. At night, darkness is the rule. No one ever lights the smallest candle, anywhere. The major part of our existence unfolds in total darkness. If someone ventures to light a fire, a tiny little fire, a deafening racket rises up, everyone protests and grumbles. Because everyone is jittery from fear of the Germans, who have become even more savage. They shoot at the sight of the slightest light. They've already killed a man and a woman in the Dutch barracks for this.

Those who are "lucky" enough to work for the Germans outside the camp tell us heartening news: Germany is at an impasse, its population suffering from endless bombing and food shortages. To be sure, the end is near. But here, the German soldiers and officers haven't changed—same arrogance, same brutality, same cruelty.

We are told that the Balkans have been liberated. According to this same news, a federation of Balkan republics has been created, with Salonica as its capital. And we hear many more such fantastic things as well. Even if it's not all true, on the whole, the basic state of things they describe is or will be true, that's for certain.

I'm trying to imagine the homeland liberated, with a perspective of boundless joy in a new society; it's making me dizzy. Considering things from the perspective of the deplorable state we've been reduced to, I wonder if our nerves will stand up to so much happiness. Our emotions will erupt as though from the depths of a volcano; long stifled tears would begin to flow, flow.... This happiness would be too strong, too violent. It would cause too much suffering.

But even so, we'll be able to take it. And with time, everything will return to normal, will crystallize. The nightmare will have given way to clear, healthy sensations. Beauty will become natural. Oh, this will come about, without a doubt, it must come about— even if not for me personally. But it must come about, overall, no matter for whom ... but it's sure to come, that's the important thing.

3

I thought it was the end, that I wouldn't have anything more to write down.... But there is no end. There isn't one. The days follow one after the other—dark, terrible, terrifying days. We would like to see the end, whatever it may be.

Starvation is everywhere; each of us is nothing more than a shadow. The food we receive gets scarcer each day. For three days we haven't seen a piece of bread. Some people have saved theirs and now they open up their miserable provisions and everything is moldy. Bread is gold. You can get anything with bread; you will risk everything for bread. And there are more and more thieves, especially at night. Someone suggested we take turns staying up and keeping watch so we could catch them. The hunt lasted two nights in the densest darkness. It was very dramatic, very noisy. No one slept and the results were nil.

Anyone who has a little bit of bread keeps it under his pillow or rather makes a pillow out of it. That way they feel more secure when they sleep. The mothers, especially, resort to this method to ensure a few mouthfuls for their children. As for the workers who are out working all day, they're forced to lug their entire stock with them everywhere in their bag. And their entire stock means six days' rations, at most, which is about half a loaf. The temptation is strong. Everyone ends up at some point eating the entire six days' worth in one day.

Yesterday, on the way to work (in the women's *commando*), we saw potatoes on the road; they had probably fallen from a truck or been thrown out by people from the last transport during a too long and painful march, when you prefer to run the risk of dying of hunger so as not to die of fatigue. We know all about this. And so, with our famished eyes, we caught sight of a few potatoes. One of us bent down to pick one up. But she had to drop it immediately, frightened by the savage screams of the soldier accompanying us who couldn't tolerate so much gluttony....

It's been over a month and a half since the Germans eliminated all services within the camp. Everyone has to work outside the camp in the different commandos. They don't spare anyone. Everyone outside—including the elderly and fourteen-year-old children—everyone is forced to labor. No one is in charge of keeping the blocks of the camps clean and in order. The Germans couldn't care less about it. No schools, no cleaners. Everything has plunged into chaos, into a whirlwind of dirt and rot.

In order to mobilize the maximum number of internees possible for all kinds of work, the Germans have multiplied their terror tenfold. Each day, before dawn, at four o'clock in the morning, everyone must be up. We feel hunted. A feverish coming and going, marked by anguish and terror.... It's the middle of winter; it's bitterly cold. At five o'clock, the human columns must already be in perfect order in the *Appellplatz*. This is the first *Appell* of the day (*Arbeitsappell*—roll call for work). It's still completely dark out, we stand for at least two hours waiting for the officer in charge who has to count us and send us off to work. Frozen, extremely weakened, famished, we feel our strength abandon us. But no leaving the square, no moving, even.

Due to the icy cold and starvation, many faint and collapse to the ground. Twice, I myself became violently dizzy and nearly succumbed. At such times, the ground has a magical appeal. Oh, how nice it would be to rest! But I managed to gather myself one more time. Falling ill here is not a good thing. No one and nothing in the world can help us. We die, and that's it.

The German officer finally deigns to count us at seven or seven thirty. He begins with a hearty volley of insults and cursing directed at everyone, he starts to let fly, kicking people for no reason, randomly. Afterwards, he chooses his victims, those who dare to explain why they can't work. These are the ones he "sets right." Systematically, he lunges at them, gives them a back-breaking beating, drags them on the ground, and tramples them—after which he forces them to stand up and take their place in the ranks.

B. B. | December 1944

The camp commander was just dismissed. Kramer was appointed in his place. Kramer, however, is the former commander of Auschwitz. Ominous reminder. All commentary is useless…. The camp regime gets more atrocious by the day. Beatings are commonplace; punishments that in the past were given to individuals and meant depriving one person of bread or of food are now collective measures meted out to the camp as a whole. What difference does it make if there are small children and sick people among us?…

An atrocious fright has gripped all of our hearts. We feel that no one looks after us any longer. We are completely at the mercy of the new commander, a villain and avowed anti-Semite. Absolute Master of the camp, he is subordinate to no one. No authority exists for us, except him. God Himself is powerless here.

Kramer does what he likes. Endless transports keep pouring in. Processions of strange creatures move constantly between the blocks and the barbed wire. Pitiful, their terrifying appearance so unlike that of human beings. Ghosts. They look at us with fright and we look at them the same way. Without a doubt we make the same impression on them as they do on us. There isn't enough room for all these people. We change places every day, each time more tightly squeezed together. Finally, they give the order that we are to sleep two to a bed, so the three-tiered bunks now contain six people. The space between the bunks is even narrower than before. This is how we emptied half of our barracks to make room for new arrivals.

Mud, rain, and dampness have moved into the barracks with us; these barracks are very poorly constructed, shabby, fissured. But there's nothing we can do about it, we have to stay here. We are submerged in an ocean of germs, lice, and fleas, of mold and stench. Literally piled one on top of the other, we form an ideal breeding ground for lice. There is no way to chase them away or eliminate them. The rock of Sisyphus. Moving around has become impossible. As for sitting or lying down to rest, it is out of the question. Hellish crowding ... what torment! One look at Barracks 25, where the French women live with the Hungarians, etc. ... pell-mell.... It's enough to drive you mad. A veritable den of thieves, as the French say. Isn't this the height of calamity that can befall us? Or can it get worse yet?

B. B. | December 1944

Kramer dismissed the Jewish camp commander. The Jews will no longer have a say in the blocks. All the administration members are disgraced. To be frank, they were all corrupt, insensitive to the group's misery, completely indifferent and thoughtless. Their role was confined to robbing others cruelly, benefitting from their position for personal gain, currying the Germans' favors by mistreating their brothers and forcing them to work for the Germans. Their behavior was scandalous in every way. But I've already spoken about them elsewhere. And besides, that's a chapter in itself.

What is important to us at the moment is Kramer and his band. He has imposed a new command on us, composed of Aryans, common criminals (the *Häftlinge*) of German, Polish, or French nationality. They are well-fed types, big and strong as bulls. They continually strut among us with clubs, beating whomever they wish. They wear convicts' clothes, those striped pants and long shirts with large numbers marked on the back. But the most tragic thing is that by their very nature, they are criminals in the worst sense of the word. Their body and soul sold to the devil—to Kramer—they have nothing of humanity left in them. Cynical, cruel, sadistic. You should see the perverse joy they take in beating people. I've noticed it clearly. They are wild animals disguised as men. This is what the Germans have done, what they have reduced them to. And it seems that it is on us that they intend to take their revenge.

These hardened criminals are our masters from this moment on, free to dispose of our lives, our souls, our children. We are enslaved under these vile serfs. What an infernal scheme! The Nazi brute is never short of ideas when it comes to finding a way to humiliate man better, to crush him better. The new command, these new *Kapos* attack the male internees especially. They persecute them mercilessly. There is a place called the *Stuppenkommando*. It's the death commando. In the evening, after work, not one of the men who have worked there returns unscathed. There they are beaten to the point of being broken, bloody, and swollen. Yesterday, December 30, two men died under their bludgeons. The same day, two others were brought back to the camp on stretchers carried by their comrades. The "kapos" also strike the women or, worse yet, succeed in prostituting them.

B. B. | January 1945

The new regime weighs on us like a nightmare. The "kapos" are like warped, drunken, insane, bloodthirsty beasts. There is no news, nothing that can bring us back to life. A deadly silence. In this horrifying terror, all has become mute. We don't see an end to it.

B. B. | January 1945

I succeeded in talking to some of the women from the transport that came from Auschwitz. Most of them are Jewish women from Poland, Greece, or Hungary. They tell us what they've experienced at Auschwitz. In 1943 and 1944 alone, during the time they were there, hundreds of thousands of people were exterminated. They are among the few hundred who miraculously managed to get out of there.

"There are no words to describe what we went through," they tell us. And they tell us of mass murders, by gas, of 99 percent of the detainees who were eliminated in this way, of their executioners' depraved behavior. They tell us all this while scrutinizing us to see if we believe them; because, they say, they are beginning themselves to doubt the truth of what they say. They fear that no one will ever believe them, that their words will be taken as those of aberrant, demented people. Only a few hundred women remain alive out of all those who were deported to Auschwitz. The men and the children were immediately eliminated, as were the elderly and the weak. A Jewish woman from Greece tells me that out of seventy thousand Greek Jews interned at Auschwitz with her, only three hundred women are still alive. She herself saw her parents and her entire family disappear in smoke.

It's strange. These women who have escaped from hell and who worked in the kitchens, in the depots, in the orchestra, even, seem relatively healthy. They're all robust, well preserved. It's bizarre, when you compare them to our own bodies. They tell us: Back there, in Auschwitz, people got enough to eat. On top of that, the internees themselves had organized a sort of mutual assistance program and made arrangements to procure what they needed. In general, they didn't suffer from hunger. On the other hand, the risk of death hovered over everyone, each person knew he was under constant threat of a sudden, irrevocable death, as each one imagined himself already consumed by the flames....

The death factory functioned at full capacity every day. Columns of men, of women, several hundreds and sometimes even one or two thousand per day, waited their turn at the entrance to the gas showers. The crematory smoked right before their eyes, and they just watched, knowing exactly what it meant. The smoke spoke to them of the fire where their loved ones had burned and where they themselves would soon end their existence. No, they weren't hungry there, our companions from Auschwitz tell us, dismayed by our tales of the methodical hunger we are subjected to. All this just shows that the goal is the same, only the means vary. Back there, a brutal and cynical process, mass assassinations by gassing; here, a slow extermination, calculated in a cowardly way through hunger, violence, terror, consciously sustained epidemics....

B. B. | January 1945

For a long time now we have not been taken to the central baths where they used to make us take hot showers—under the impudent and jeering gaze of the soldiers in charge of watching over us. In spite of our extreme uneasiness, we were nonetheless glad to be able to be clean for a few days.

But now, nothing. No baths, no hot water. These are only dreams now. The only thing left for us is to take advantage of the camp's wash-houses, infectious, frozen. We undress en masse, all together, cramped, jostled. No point in waiting "your turn" because there are too many of us and the spigots are always taken—unless, of course, the water is turned off. We undress hastily in the bitter cold, all of us, men, women pell-mell. Nobody is embarrassed. No one pays any attention to the person washing himself next to him. Besides, sex has no meaning here. The important thing is to scrub yourself. Teeth chatter, the icy water burns the skin; it's painful, but it doesn't matter.

As for the constant hunger, our bodies have grown accustomed to it. It happens that someone who is tortured by the acute pain of hunger, who can't stand it anymore, ends up eating his entire reserve bread (three or four rations) all at once, or exchanging his clothes for one or two bowls of soup (offered by thieves).... And when he has swallowed this unusual quantity of wretched food, he feels ill, worse than before, his body protests violently. He's left with nausea, and his hunger remains unappeased.

We receive our food more and more irregularly. The noontime soup gets distributed at five or six o'clock in the evening and the evening meal (boiled water or a little piece of synthetic cheese) has been crossed off the agenda until the following morning ... or not at all. That's why we sometimes go sixteen to twenty hours with nothing. And naturally, at the first distribution after such a long wait, famished bodies throw themselves on the vats; the sad consequences are inevitable a few hours later: collective diarrhea infests the whole area.

B. B. | January 1945

The camp has been permanently invaded by fleas and all kinds of vermin, not to mention dysentery, which has taken on unheard-of proportions. The latter is caused by overall intestinal poisoning that spreads rapidly. There's no way to stop it and no cure. It literally devours the body and everything reeks, soiled and vile—the floors, the beds, the sinks, the yards, the toilets (communal holes)—a deluge.

Although we are consumed by this cholera, and dying from weakness, we all try as best we can to clean the area. A sad and useless task. It's hopeless. We feel like we are nearly insane. So many exhausted, famished, half-dead bodies reduced to skeletons. And so much excrement.

B. B. | January 1945

Starvation is everywhere. We only manage to move with great difficulty. No one can walk straight anymore. Everyone staggers or drags their feet. Entire families die in a matter of days. The elderly Mrs. M. died quickly; two days later her husband died. Then came their children's deaths, devoured by famine and fleas. One of them, a nearsighted young boy, couldn't kill the vermin that had settled on his body because he couldn't see them; they've burrowed deep into his skin and swarmed through his eyebrows. His chest is completely blackened by these thousands of fleas and their nests.

We have never seen such a thing; we never imagined such a thing could occur. The poor boy is completely destroyed and dazed by it; already he seems like an imbecile. People say that he was once an extremely intelligent boy. Today, his bony, thin body drags itself feebly from one end of the barracks to the other, groaning and wailing. Everyone avoids him. His brothers and sister dread his presence, his fleas, his howling, and take care not to go near him. The other night, he dragged his useless body from one bed to the other until the morning, begging people to make room for him. Everyone pushed him away in disgust. Besides, there are already two people in each bed. No one wants to be his "partner" and there are no empty beds. So young M. is dying with nowhere to rest his body.

Painful story. His case is not unique. There are thousands of similar cases in the camp. Especially among the elderly. Their fate is dreadful. A bleak, odious, undignified end awaits them all: this slow, painful process of death by the decay and rot of their own bodies.

B. B. | January 1945

Death has moved in to stay. It's our most loyal tenant. Always and ever present. Men die en masse due to vile treatment, hunger, humiliation, dysentery, and vermin. They fall, they collapse. Their number diminishes rapidly. Many of my acquaintances ended their lives in this manner. Every morning we find one or two corpses in the beds. One, two, three, four.... We end up confusing the living and the dead. Because in essence the difference between them is minimal; we are skeletons who still possess some capacity to move, they are immobile skeletons.

There is yet a third category: those who still breathe a little but remain lying down, unable to move. We wait for them to pass, to make room for others. It's not surprising that we confuse them with the dead and that we lose count.

The epitome of wretchedness is when they make us change barracks. And lately they force us to move two or three times every month. All the misery, all the human decay, all the tattered clothes, the rags, the cumbersome and useless packages ... the moaning of sick people too numerous to take care of, the death rattle of the dying thrown outside in the whirlwind of the move, in the hubbub of swearing, arguments, complaints. This entire immense tragedy suffocated till now in the foul depths of the barracks ... all of this, at once, is exposed in the open air, in the mire and rain, in insanity. Thus, completely exposed beneath a pale, impassive sky, all this becomes infinitely more sorrowful and atrocious.

As a general rule, these moves cost us a surplus of several deaths over and above the norm. This forced dragging about is real torment for those of us who are relatively healthy, while for the sick and the aged it means certain death.

B. B. | February 1945

Typhoid fever rules over us. For the moment, it's the children in particular who succumb to it. But the children die of other illnesses and we never know exactly of what. A diagnosis would be very complicated anyway. Two young girls, very cute, died one "fine" morning in a bed near ours.... Just like that, one a few hours after the other. Their mother, a very pretty and simple young woman, had watched them and taken care of them like a she-wolf with her babies. Seeing them dead, she was gripped by such violent pain that her screams were ear-splitting. Then she started to sing lamentations, inventing lines with incredible talent, and to chat softly with her two dead little girls. Now she drags herself around, her hair disheveled, constantly in rags, horribly neglected, madness in her eyes. Life clearly has no more meaning for her....

B. B. | February 1945

I was on duty two nights in a row in the older women's barracks. Since nearly all of them are sick, they never leave their beds. These two nights were dreadful. The first thing to say is that the work is done in complete darkness because of the bomb alerts, and that it amounts to calming the women's anguish, distributing bedpans, then emptying them in the nearby toilets. The air is completely foul.

These sick old women lie down, slowly dying; they rot alive. I don't know how else to say it. And yet, they show such a will to live, it's unbelievable. They never stop lamenting and asking for help. Sometimes, they really get on my nerves. For the most part they are women who come from well-to-do bourgeois milieus from Western Europe (Holland, Belgium, France), and in the past they were accustomed to living in comfort, surrounded by attention. They are totally incapable of understanding their current situation, completely unaware of the current reality ... which makes them impossible sometimes. Yet they seem so wretched!

I thread my way between the narrow beds, crumpling their lace, an entire ocean of useless and smelly lace, relics of their former luxury. And I do my best to straighten up the places where they lie, to help them wash their faces. These living corpses, these jaundiced faces of ghosts struggling in spasms of agony—it is all truly horrible, and everything takes place in utter darkness.

I am a permanent prisoner of wretchedness and horror. The first night, three of the patients died. I had to lay out their corpses and cover them. A corpse is heavy, and I have hardly any strength left in me.... Nonetheless, dealing with the dead didn't frighten me in any way. We see them in every corner of this place. We "live" together; we are numb to it.

The second night, I waged a genuine battle with a crazy woman, Frau Polak. I had to subdue her to stop her from scaring and hitting the other women in the dark, as she was in the habit of doing. Three times during the night, she jumped from her bed and each time, I had to stop her. This is not simple at all. She has a way of imploring you, of moaning—it's appalling. Moreover, she does not seem stupid if you discount her bouts of insanity. She's just a horribly unhappy woman. People say she used to be quite intelligent. But then, after a series of "unexpected" misfortunes from which the war did not spare her, she slowly and progressively began to lose her mind ... and today she's completely mad. The only thing she ever does is to explain something to me and to try with all her might to convince me her arguments are sound. There's nothing mean in what she says. It's just that everything she says bears the distinctive mark of despair and entreaty. On the other hand, there are three genuinely hysterical women among the sick who are frankly frightening.

These nights spent in this hellish barracks have set my nerves on edge. I felt suddenly as though I had aged ten years. The shock was so violent that it took me several days to recover from it.

B. B. | February 1945

The new regime under the direction of the criminals has only encouraged the corruption that has long been rampant in the entire camp. It's only natural, of course. When the great change of power occurred, when control of the camp passed from the hands of the Jews to those of the *Kapos*, the main thieves and those who had reigned as masters over the rest of us for several months became suddenly silent, withdrawn. But that only lasted a short while. They were lying in wait and quickly figured out that things were going to take a good turn for them. Better than ever, even.

The terrain turned out to be ideal.... And now here they are, back on the attack: they rapaciously steal everything that falls into their hands and torment the others disgracefully. They were quick to come to an agreement with their new masters, the *Häftlinge*, with their help they have organized an intense black market and, on condition that the *Häftlinge* return the favor, have become their right-hand men in the bloodthirsty attacks on the internees. This is what goes on under our very eyes in our barracks. And it's exactly the same in the other barracks. Traitors, villains who deserve to hang.

They are constantly chewing on something; they gorge themselves on the finest delicacies completely inconsiderately, under the moribund gaze of a crowd of famished corpses. Degenerate monsters.... They have overstepped all bounds. "Fate" has smiled on them and they are crazed. They insult everyone, fear no one, have no hesitations. They brutally beat and threaten all who dare make a comment, to report them to the *Kapos*. The first chance they get, they take revenge by delivering the "nuisances" to the mercy of the *Kapos* who arrive every morning to send people off to forced labor. And the scoundrels hasten zealously to facilitate this heinous process for them. It's thanks to them that the *Häftlinge* always succeed in finding new victims for the work details. Those famous *Kommandos* of terror and death.

There are no words to describe the cruelty of these decadent traitors, these abject serfs in the pay of criminals, these gravediggers thirsty for human blood....

Everyone thinks only of himself. No one feels anything for anyone else. Many women have given in. Young girls who've known nothing of life or its foundations have heedlessly seized what these pitiful circumstances offer them and have yielded. Carousing, flirting, drinking, dancing, singing, laughing out loud, wearing silk stockings and beautiful dresses—this is their lifestyle here, in league with the *Kapos*.

Hunger crushes the spirit. I feel my physical and intellectual strength diminishing. Things escape me, I can't think properly, can't grasp events, can't realize the full horror of the situation. Only once in a while, in moments as brief as a flash of lightening, a clear and precise thought crosses my mind and I wonder: what is this dark, perverse, underhanded force that succeeds in hurling humanity as a whole into such absurd and abominable conditions?

B. B. | February 1945

I share my bed with Mrs. G., a fairly corpulent woman in her fifties who has been literally immobilized by disease, hunger, and nicotine. Confined to her bed, heavy and inert like lead, she never gets up. All day long, I don't know what to do with my body; I can't get the slightest space in this damned bed to rest my slowly atrophying limbs a little. Breathing has become nearly impossible for me, too.

In the evening, I sink into our shared, damp hole on the lowest level of a bed whose two upper levels are occupied by three adults and two children. Our bed is right next to the wall, or rather, those worm-eaten planks that rain seeps through ceaselessly. The window and the door are also nearby. The dampness has penetrated everywhere, soaking everything, clothing, bodies, blankets.... Things aren't damp here, they're drenched. Water and mud everywhere, inside and out. And along with them, the air saturated by the suffocating odor exhaled by those suffering from typhus and the stench of urine. Is this a bed? Call it what you want, but not a bed. A muddy swamp.

Climbing out of this hole in the morning, my face is completely swollen, my eyelids are sealed, and it takes an hour or two for me to be able to open my eyes and see clearly around me. Each time I wonder if I've gone blind. This is certainly not a bed, it's a tomb—a tomb built for two.

B. B. | February 1945

On the twelfth of this month it will be a year since we were arrested in Cetinje. Vain hopes and foolish predictions filled most of our time. In the beginning, we rejoiced because we were nearly convinced that everything would be over soon. Enormous deception, because in those days the war was at its height. So now we have become skeptical. These long, fateful winter months, dominated by anguish, famine, vermin, terror, and death, offer no encouragement.

Oh, hunger, hunger … is there anything in the world more appalling, more demeaning for man? I am haunted by these faces of animals in agony, crowding desperately around a few vats containing lukewarm, fetid, bitter water that is called soup.… Because now, what we get by way of soup is water in which a few pieces of already rotted rutabagas have been boiled. This is often done two full days before they distribute it. The vats are immediately filled, then hermetically sealed (so as to "keep the soup hot") to be opened only one or two days later at the time for distribution. So the entire contents quickly spoils. And we are served.…

There was a time, we remember, when rutabagas, whether boiled or raw, delighted us. We were as hungry as bears. Now, our hunger has only become fiercer. Our bodies have been demolished by it, we all drag ourselves around like rags; men literally drop to the ground from exhaustion and end up dying of hunger, simple as that. And yet, no one touches that soup anymore, no one is able to swallow it. As soon as it arrives, it gets thrown on the trash heaps that accumulate rapidly everywhere and give off acidic fumes.

Fascinating and strange news sometimes reaches our ears ... but now it seems like it has nothing to do with us. Sounds from another world, from beyond our graves....

All that we know, all that we see is the slow, uninterrupted flow of long processions of miserable creatures, thousands and thousands of internees flocking here from the various camps the Germans were forced to evacuate. There is no doubt about it: the Germans are beating their retreat, dragging their victims with them. And piling them up in here. Rumor has it that we, too, will end up being removed from here, that the Allies are close by and the Germans will soon evacuate this area and send us elsewhere. All these rumors, all this uncertainty, along with the possibility that in the end they will kill us all (and Kramer's presence serves as a confirmation of this), it all adds up to such moral torment that more than once we have felt on the edge of insanity.

And the wretched lines follow one after the other, endlessly, all along the road ... skeletons. From the other side of the barbed wire, we watch them pass by, wondering who they are. And what will be done with them? What is wanted from us? How will they end up? And we? What is happening? What are they waiting for? What about the British? What do they want? What are their plans? They control the situation—are they making a game of the whole world, maintaining the state of affairs that best suits them? Otherwise, they could have defeated Germany a long time ago....

These human lives, the torture, death, and putrefaction of slaves, what difference does all this make to them? None. Freedom. A bluff, as long as this works for them. Exploiters of the common people, they are, favored, privileged in the current hierarchy of nations. That's why things are as they are. The only thing that counts is the policy of the USSR and faith in the triumph of the new society. Otherwise, what good is all this? Is war a part of human nature? What does it all mean? If there is no true victory, if the whole world doesn't become socialist, then what good is all this? More massacres, more putrefaction? I am beginning to despair for mankind.

We want so many things, we hunger for so much. Is this really our end? And what about the Jewish question? Where and how will this hellish drama end? In our Jewish homeland? Where and why? How? What form will it take? Where are our destinies truly to end? Never before have such thoughts tormented me. Never before have I asked myself such questions. And now, I have the feeling that this is something eternal. An incurable wound. Our beloved Slavic homeland, how we love you. But will you want us? Will we be strangers for you, too? I feel like I've lost my mind, indeed, what idiocy, what absurd questions.

B. B. | March 1945

Everything we see here, everything that happens under our eyes makes us begin to question our own human qualities. A dark and heavy doubt awakens. Doubt in mankind. And we begin to ask ourselves some strange questions. Just yesterday, in fact, I had a long discussion with Professor K. He's in the "hospital," totally exhausted, his limbs and face completely swollen with chilblains and edema. Wounds all over his body do not heal. And along with that, dysentery that torments him, all sorts of other pain. I come to see him regularly to help him out and to alleviate his suffering in some small way. And we discuss the great misfortune that has struck us. We remain perplexed, wondering if it's possible to believe in a normal life after all that we have lived through here. Nearly impossible.... This is, it seems, our end, a disgraceful, atrociously disgraceful *finale* to our existence.

We analyze the behavior of certain people.... Everyone "manages" as they can. The question necessarily comes up: could all this be just one enormous test? One way to determine to what extent so and so possesses "a sense of direction," a "talent for life"? Is that what this is? The talent for life? The struggle with death, an instinct for self-preservation? All these acts of disloyalty and corruption that evince a complete lack of scruples, these acts of cynical pillage carried out in all conscience to the detriment of some famished phantoms...is this an instinct for self-preservation? Is this the criteria for individual strength and vigor? Must man become a brute, a ferocious beast, in order to remain alive?

And so the result would be that those of us who do not know how to "struggle" in this manner and don't turn to beastly measures are inept at life and doomed to ruin? I have no idea. Could this be the supreme law of nature, of all living creatures? So it would seem, fine, but then what? What about human reason? Doesn't that count for anything? The human mind created ethical ideas and laws to counteract and strive against animalistic laws dictated solely by instinct. What have these ethical ideas and laws become? Have they no say here?

Oh, but I am firmly and deeply persuaded that those for whom ethical principles represent primordial laws, those for whom these ethical principles are second nature and really have become their "human instinct," an instinct that has taken the place of animal instinct in the bestial struggle that rages on around them—those people are not doomed to disappear completely, they will not perish, they will not succumb. I am equally convinced that I too will preside over my own situation in the end by maintaining my principles, by allowing my humanity to triumph ... as long as my health continues to serve me as wonderfully as it has up to this point. So here we are, it's a matter of health, of physical resistance; it's to this objective fact that I owe having been able to maintain a certain moral bearing in human dignity. So it's not a question of personal merit. I don't know what to think anymore....

We continue our discussion. Who is right and who is wrong? How should one behave? Let's analyze: J. and his morality, L. and his reasoning, Li. and his tactics, R. and his logic, the K. family and their spirit of compromise. Along with all these, let's broach the subject a little: the art of giving—where does the "right" for some to give out charity and for others to receive it come from? There is good reason, too, to explain a little the root of I's truly amazing business skills that, in the present circumstances, become particularly revolting.

Professor K. considers that ethics, such as we conceive of them, are out of place and incompatible with this concentration camp. To hear him tell it, ethics are just useless and you have to disregard them if you want to survive in spite of it all in order to be able to, afterward, contribute to the creation of a world where these ethics will be the rule. The mind is subordinate to matter, it is only its emanation, matter sublimated, the superstructure. Consequently, it is inevitable and bound to happen that matter will reject the mind wherever the mind is out of place and becomes an anomaly.

I don't know.... It does not enter into my head. Concretely speaking, in the cases we are considering here, what does matter's victory really mean, in essence? It simply means making compromises with the enemy, betraying your principles, denying your soul to save your body. Pushing this logic even further with concrete examples, it means flirting with the executioners, prostituting yourself and lowering your eyes like a coward in the face of calamity and massive death, eating what you stole from others, and doing the rounds over a pile of corpses. It means selling your human judgment, your dignity, and your principles. It means, in short, saving your skin at the expense of others' skin.... But after all, is one man's life of such value that he should be allowed to commit all these horrors to preserve himself?

B. B. | March 1945

We all have typhoid fever and are bedridden. They put a special barbed wire fence around our barracks. Quarantine was put in place. The fever consumed me for two weeks. First my fever was at 41, then 40 degrees, then 39, and 38. No medication. Whoever can make it will. During those two weeks I had dreadful headaches and constant nausea. The feeling of hunger had completely disappeared. I was delirious. The only thing I felt was that death was close by, very close by, not just all around, but right next to me this time. I felt its breath inside me.

I was slowly and consciously dying. My body felt nothing and seemed to quietly cease to function. Persistent, only the idea of death was alive in me. Around me, everyone was dying as well, and they continue to die, each one in turn. I am now in a bed on the second level. Mrs. K. is below me; in one month she lost her husband and her daughter.... full of grief, in silence, she returned to her bed, lay down and is waiting her turn. She moans continuously even though she no longer feels any real pain, of that I am certain. She just can't take it anymore; she wants nothing more from life. It's her life, her miserable existence that hurts her. She gets impatient; she wants it to be over with, that's all.

Above me is C. Completely dazed, all he does is yell, trying at all costs to persuade the others that he is neither sick nor crazy, neither foul-smelling nor infected. On my right, two elderly men, F. and K., passed away. One night, for hours, half awake, I followed the final agony of one of them ... And the following night, I clearly heard the death rattle of the other. That's how it is: the breathing stops, either in this person or that person. No one is in a position to help anyone else. The corpses remain stretched out on the beds next to the living or the half-dead. The living and the dead ... all are mixed together. There is almost nothing that distinguishes them from each other; there is almost no difference.

Facing death and the dead ... complete indifference. It has become so commonplace. No one thinks about liberation anymore, no one counts the days as we used to.... It's tiresome.... What good is it knowing when the Allies are supposed to arrive, even though they are known to be only a few kilometers from here? What does it matter? For the moment, only death is our closest and most faithful ally. And if someone does start counting the days from time to time, it's not to try to calculate the hour of liberation, but rather how long one or another of us will last. It's like a medical curiosity for everyone. A strange obsession. Not so long ago I claimed I would live another month or two.... But now, after the attack of typhoid fever that I have miraculously survived but that has depleted what was left of my strength, now I don't expect to live more than one and a half to two weeks at most.

I am spending my remaining semi-existence in the company of other ghosts, living and dead. The corpses—the real ones—are still here with us, in our beds. There's no one to remove them. And nowhere to put them. Everything is full. In the courtyards, too, the corpses pile up, heaps of corpses. They rise higher and higher each day. The crematory can't burn them all.

The food doesn't come at all anymore. From time to time, a vat of sour soup. Sometimes we cut a weed and boil it. We pick potato skins out of the trash. Those who have sold themselves still possess something, but they have no resistance against the contagion, the agony, or death either. It's a general thing, suspended in the air, imminent for everyone.

No one checks on us. The Germans don't show up anymore. We know that their end is near, very near. But so is ours. And they know it, too. They have nothing more to do with this camp, which is why they don't set foot in it anymore. Once they completed the hellish task they were assigned and that some accomplished quite well, they withdrew leaving us here to die until the last one.

The *Kapos* continue to strut around and beat people. It's monstrous. Among them, there are some who take pity on us ... at times. I've seen it. But it's only by chance. In general, they only watch us cynically and don't stop sneering at our expense.

B. B. | April 1945

I am terribly ashamed to have lived through all this. Men are rotting and decomposing in the mud. There are reports that in one of the neighboring blocks acts of cannibalism have arisen. According to a personal statement by a German doctor who finally came to our block to take stock of the "progress" of mass deaths—according to his statement, then, over the past two months, February and March, more than seventeen thousand internees per month died—that is to say, thirty-five thousand out of forty-five thousand internees.

If only they had been simple, humane deaths.... Ah, no, I don't want to die like this. I don't want to! It would be better to die right away, as quickly as possible ... like a human being. What? Allow your body and soul to putrefy and to wallow in their own filth, to slowly but irrevocably disappear from total starvation, to sink into nothingness, devoured by pus and stench and going through all the stages of decomposition before rotting to death? Because that's exactly what it is: we don't die here, we rot to death. Why wait? That would be an affront to human dignity. What a disgrace, what an immense disgrace....

I look at this gloomy barracks full of ghosts, humiliation, hatred, these motionless sick people reduced to total powerlessness, these living and already putrefied corpses ... a dark abyss where an entire humanity founders.... Oh, no, as long as my brain can function normally, I will not allow myself to end like this. It is man's duty to die like a man, to avoid a death worse than all deaths, a death that isn't a death.

B. B. | April 1945

It's awful, what they have done to mankind. The darkest scenes from the Middle Ages or the Inquisition are reproduced and multiplied here to the extreme. Their monstrous "revival" will forever leave the mark of shame and infamy on the "civilized" and "cultured" Germany of the twentieth century.

This darkest and most degrading slavery imaginable has made it so that life in this camp has nothing in common with life as humans conceive it.

It is indeed a cruel plan aiming to cause the systematic and certain end of thousands of human lives. Of that, *there is not the slightest doubt, not the slightest doubt.* It requires nothing but to see clearly and to follow attentively everything that goes on in order to deduce, with no hesitation: this camp is not made to hold civilian deportees or prisoners of war for a specific period of time, to temporarily deprive them of freedom for whatever political, diplomatic, or strategic reasons with the intention of holding them and releasing them alive before or after the cessation of hostilities.... No: this camp is consciously and knowingly organized and arranged in such a way as to methodically exterminate thousands of human beings according to a plan. If this continues for only one more month, it is highly doubtful that one single person among us will come through.

On my parents

I do not associate my father's death with the "final solution" years. I was surprised and relieved to discover this after sitting at his bedside for two days as he lay dying. The ghetto—placed as it is on the genocide assembly line, its head in Germany and its far-reaching edges spread apart like an octopus's tentacles—did not impose itself on me as some sort of prologue to his death.

This was quite the opposite of how I had expected to feel, considering the constant presence of those years in my interactions with my parents during their lifetime.

It was what it was: the death of a seventy-four-year-old man who neglected his health, although in his latter years he did show signs (to my surprise as well) of loving life.

His dying in July 1997 was my dress rehearsal for my mother's dying four years later, in June 2001. She was then eighty-eight, yearning to die, but death tarried.

This essay was originally written in Ramallah in December 2005. It was first published in Hebrew in February 2007 in *Mitaam*, an Israeli leftist literary quarterly.

He lay dying for a day and a half after his stroke. My mother's death came three days after being released from a week at the hospital, although the doctors told me she could live on like that (with oxygen, having trouble breathing) for a long time. But her resolve was different—refusing food, drink, medication, and finally, in her last thirty hours, refusing to speak. ("I am like the French," she used to quote a French saying in order to tease me when I thought she talked too much and told tall tales. "The fact that I have nothing to say doesn't mean I have to keep quiet.") With her Bosnian obstinacy, as I used to call it, she lifted her chin, clamped her teeth shut, and would neither eat nor drink in those last days.

Both of them talked a lot and said much in their last days. Both of them moved back and forth from crystal clarity to vague rambling. Neither of them, again contrary to my expectations, mentioned the ghetto (Shorgorod in Transniestria, where Abraham Hass was exiled from his hometown of Suceava, Romania, with his family and hundreds of thousands of Jews from Bukovina in 1941), nor Bergen-Belsen death camp (where Hanna Lévy was sent in summer 1944, after half a year in a Gestapo prison in Montenegro). With both of them I made the same inevitable mistake: I did not pose urgent last questions, nor did I hurriedly record anything they said in those last moments. Thus, I entrusted their words to memory and remained with questions that would never be answered. Now I realize how reluctant I was to stage the reality, to play a role in a farewell at a deathbed scene, to turn them into objects of a documenting fashion, to do what they themselves had refrained from doing.

For their own reasons, they did not leave behind them neat records of their lives and thoughts. Abraham did try to jot things down here and there, writing in a Hebrew that sounded to me more and more like some longing for Yiddish. He promised himself that I would eventually edit his memoirs, but got stuck. He probably cringed at the prospect of sounding self-important ("He loves himself too much"—this was one of the worst things he would say about anyone). Hanna, who wrote beautifully and was fluent in several languages, refused to write anything beyond the diary she kept in Bergen-Belsen from 1944 to 1945, the writing of which would have been punishable by death on the spot. "So many books are being written," she countered when I begged her to write. "If one has nothing really extraordinary to say—there is no sense in writing." For me this was another facet of her utter lack of ambition, giving up any thought of doing something special with her life and talents.

I conclude that her resignation set in after the war, upon her return from Bergen-Belsen to Belgrade. After all, before the war she enjoyed her studies at the university and the independent life she consciously chose as a teacher. What role did depression play in her lack of ambition, the mental condition that haunted her for the rest of her life? How crucial were circumstances? In the Introduction, I already mentioned the several disapointments she encountered upon returning to the "new" Belgrade. There is another incident that might have played a key role in the abrupt decisions she made.

A photo of Tito that fell off the wall as she passed it in the government office where she worked raised a storm of suspicion against the "Jewess" (also ethnically suspected of entertaining favorable sentiments toward the USSR because of Gromyko's supportive speech on the founding of the state of Israel). Was that seemingly trivial incident the last straw that pushed her to leave her homeland and emigrate? To what extent was her depression exacerbated by the fact that in Israel she found no work as a teacher at her "advanced age" of thirty-five? Was it because of being a declared communist in McCarthyist times? For all I know, her depression may have set in even before Bergen-Belsen.

The two deaths communicate with each other in my mind, commingling stories in my memory about my parents and their life stories: two Holocaust survivors seeking partnership in their own private abyss, while their closer, inner communist circle dogmatically denied that abyss, just as the outer Zionist circle arrogantly pretended to be their resurrection. Their communicating deaths are bound to their lives and thoughts as represented in my own mind. I almost wrote "complete their image and their content as represented in my mind" but "complete" is misleading in this case. Their images and lives gradually recede like a waning moon with each passing year of their absence, and with every question I raise about them and their pasts, with no one there to answer.

Moon. I allowed myself three exceptions to the inner rule not to "stage" their dying: one with my father, two with my mother.

One day at the hospital, several days before she died, I asked her to quote me the Latin epigram that teaches one how to tell whether the moon is waxing or waning. Luna lies, it says. When she is D-shaped, she waxes, and when C-shaped, she wanes. I was embarrassed to ask, lest I seem to be anticipating death. But she immediately recited the epigram, rolling her *r*'s without protest. I wrote it down in Latin but could not ask her to check my spelling. *La luna mendeas est. Si descrecet, crecet. Si crecet, decrecet.* (Luna lies. When she seems to wane, she waxes. Seeming to wax, she wanes.) I hope my request pleased her. This epigram used to serve us as a moment of relief, our own private sort of fun—she seemingly showing off her Latin studies and wondering what memory retained, conjuring up a whiff of bygone schooldays, and I, back to being the child who asks her mother to repeat her "tricks" (and she had quite a few of those, in several languages, from various periods of her life).

I also asked her then, at the hospital, to recite to me the lyrics of a lullaby she would sing to me in "Yugoslav," her mother tongue, as I thought of it, the language in which she counted, and which gave her that accent I could never imitate. (German, Russian, English, and French accents I could imitate well and used to amuse her, causing her to laugh to the point of tears when I did so.) I wrote down the lyrics in this Yugoslav language, at a time when Yugoslavia no longer existed, and "Yugoslav" was a politically incorrect term. I wrote them in Hebrew letters. And I fear she did not recall them in full, or perhaps I did not quite get all the lyrics and was too shy to ask her again and again to repeat them.

Both my parents were liberated by the Soviet Red Army. If this has left me with a soft spot for the name itself, it's no wonder that my parents always retained their affectionate sentiments toward the USSR. Hanna told me more than once about the Red Army commander whom she ran into at the German village where she spent her first night free from captivity after two years. One soldier, an ignorant dolt, suspected her of being German. His commanding officer realized that such a ragged skeleton could not possibly be German. *"Germania Vashaya,"* (Germany is all yours) he said to her as a gracious liberator, startled by her apperance (she guessed) but managing to conceal it.

Once, perhaps twenty years ago, we watched a strange film together—French I think. I don't recall its title or content. But it had a sentimental scene of Red Army soldiers dancing and singing. Before going into battle, or after it, or unrelated to battle—I have no idea. "I cried so hard, I don't know what got into me," she said, surprised at herself after that scene. She was not accustomed to crying. I suppose we both knew why she cried. Disillusioned with her dream of the USSR, longing for that dream, angry at the dream and its destroyers and at innocence at large, she still felt grateful to the peoples of the USSR for their courage, their valor.

As Abraham Hass, my father, was rushed half-paralyzed to the emergency ward, he heard the doctor's Russian accent and immediately said a few words to him in Russian. The doctor was surprised.

Perhaps the doctor supposed this mustachioed, dark-skinned man was Iraqi. Many mistook him for a Jew of Iraqi descent or some other Arab nationality, especially in his younger years. And he never even managed to pick up the guttural "a" and "h" sounds. He told me how he said to this doctor, "The Red Army liberated me, and that I shall never forget," half-paralyzed, eyes shut, head bursting with an untreated condition of high blood pressure, which the doctors were amazed to discover. "And the doctor said to me," he went on telling me with his eyes shut, "that if that was so, then not everything was bad about the Soviets." My father must have had it wrong. The doctor could not have said "Soviets," but for Abraham Hass his liberators had always remained "Soviets": an imagined identity that for him was objective, an ideological and moral identity, not ethnic. An entity of a mission, devoted to internationalist, not nationalist ideas. Like tens of millions or even more, he imposed this ideal of his on reality. Many years after 1956, when their murderousness became undeniable, he found it difficult to acknowledge the reality of these oppressive regimes, cynical, hypocritical nomenclatures, nationalism in the guise of anti-imperialism, reigns of terror, inequality, and stark exploitation of workers. He did see "mistakes," of course, in those regimes, found fault with leaders, spoke of "petrified thinking" inside the party, believed that reforms were possible. He believed in democratization, quarreled with those who remained official Stalinists over certain issues, felt close to the Italian communists. But he saw no structural failure in a system that pretended to implement communist ideology and presented it as a scientific formula for grasping the reins of power.

His shouts on the telephone woke me up to the Soviet invasion of Prague in August 1968: "They have gone too far!" or something of this sort. The house fell into mourning.

In 1977, when I spent a few months in Romania—under the most insanely tyrannical regime of Eastern Europe in the 1970s and '80s—he came for a visit. I saw his denial mechanism swing into full action. On the train from Bucharest to his hometown, Suceava, he spoke about the fascists of the 1940s, about poverty and exploitation back then, about the West that does everything in its power to undermine any attempted change, as in Chile, about the involvement of the CIA, about provocateurs. This was how he avoided my reports of oppression and massive human suffering at the hands of the Romanian Communist Party in its reign of terror.

Gradually he overcame his mental obstacle, his tunnel vision. After all, he could not deny the fact that, in the name of the Communist Party and internationalism, Ceaucescu reigned supreme as a tyrant-emperor over a terrified, impoverished, and ill populace with the full collaboration of a hypocritical, opportunistic nomenclature sporting its red flag.

I wish I could recall my father saying something very clear about the moral responsibility of anyone regarding themselves as a Marxist leftist for the existence of the monstrosities created in Eastern Europe, China, Cambodia, and North Korea, and the various Pol Pots that such regimes produced. By "leftist" I mean anyone for whom the equality of human beings is a supreme value, and nationality a fact rather than an ethical issue; those who—despite repeated defeats—have not given up seeking ways to end the exploitation of most of humanity from which certain minorities profit, amassing wealth and pleasure; those who—in spite of defeats and contradictions—have not surrendered their faith in and support of popular struggles; those for whom principles are signposts in the path of thinking, action, and conduct rather than rigid religious-like laws that sanctify all means. But my memory founders regarding even one such conversation. He had made comments whose integral mass was much greater than the sum of their words, and from which I would like to conclude that he did carry on such an inner dialogue. "Now," he said, after the collapsing Eastern European regimes did away with the last remnants of his denial of reality, "the time has come to give new terms to those old feelings." On another occasion he said that "the failure of the socialist experiment does not exonerate capitalism and its inherent exploitation." He also said in Russian, *"Davai snachala!"* (Let's start over).

This was a sort of private code in our family, and I am not sure of its origin. I seem to remember their quoting Shmuel Mikunis, the Russian-born former secretary general of the Israel Communist Party, who said this after 1956, or perhaps 1968. I do not remember and have no one to ask about it, but whenever we meant it was time yet again to push the Sisyphean boulder uphill, we would say—spurring ourselves on in what seemed self-irony—*"Davai snachala!"*

In my memory it was easier for my mother not to suppress that which the so-called socialist regimes had created in her name. "I was a fool," she said when we spoke about the Communist Party, about the USSR. Sometimes she said, "We were fools" of herself and her peers. Unlike Abraham, she did not seek extenuating circumstances.

But on the last May Day of her life—in 2001, as the eighth month of the Second Intifada began, forty days before she died, (when, as had become my daily custom, I sneaked away from the ritual shooting in Ramallah between Israeli soldiers and armed Palestinians to visit her at the home for the elderly in Motza where she spent her last three years)—she waited for me outside her room. She was already breathing very heavily, but could not understand why I was so upset and worried about it. The reduced supply of oxygen to her brain accounted for her drowsiness, I suppose, her growing confusion and failing short-term memory. As always, I bent down toward her easy chair to kiss her soft, smooth cheeks. "Turn your other cheek," I used to tease her about her embarrassment at the many kisses. As she turned her other cheek, she looked up at me and said, excited: "Do you know what day it is? It's the first of May." She did not have to tell me what that day meant to her. Her belonging to a transnational community, transcending time and borders, a sense of belonging and honor to all those struggling for self-evident matters that had once been not at all self-evident, and as such were not self-evident quite yet.

My memory—impaired as I have already hinted—tells me that she mistrusted dogmas quite early on and thus taught me to distinguish between leftist essence and the authoritarian shapes it took in communist-Stalinist, Maoist, and Trotskyist movements. Her early attraction to socialist feminism, and her rancor at phallocrats—including leftist ones—equipped her with better tools than my father to begin asking questions. Familiarity with the domestic suppression of women party members cracked the communist tradition of male-leader worship (and of female leaders who did not assign any significance to male suppressive dominance). I do not know how much she dared argue at party cell meetings. I suppose not too much. But her dissidence was reinforced by her objective condition as a woman aware of the suppression of women in a conservative communist party. This helped me balance the natural and contagious tendency to believe in a paradise (such as that portrayed in Soviet children's books and films).

Her last week in the hospital taught me how much feminist thinking had empowered her. The doctors tried to explain her exhaustion, confusion, internal bleeding, breathing difficulties, insomnia, constant nightly sighing, talking to herself. For hours she was hostile to me, rehashing a mother's old resentments toward her daughter, hours of invoking old suspicions of me and my intentions. Two to three days later these were all gone, to my relief, and I was once again her "Amiritza" and "Dushitza" ("little soul" in Yugoslav). I was constantly on guard to prevent any invasive treatment by the doctors. This was the least I could do. "Help me die," she had asked more than once. I do not remember whether she repeated this in the end, at the hospital. But I asked, "How? Force a pillow over your face?" I do not remember when or where, but I do recall her waving her hands as was her habit whenever we argued, as though saying half-joking, half earnestly: "Stop it already, you nag."

When she was tired of lying in bed, I helped her sit up. Her feet hardly reached her slippers. I vividly remember one of those occasions at the hospital, sitting and talking, her eyes shut. She often spoke with her eyes shut. To help her concentrate, she always said. Behind the screens we could hear other women in the room talking: they discussed dishes they prepared for their grandchildren, talked of this singer and of that TV anchor, and in between it all they spoke of the Palestinian "murderers." I spared her the report of a suicide attack that took place at a Tel Aviv dancehall on the day I took her to Hadassah Hospital. All of a sudden she started carrying on about the success of the feminist movement and ideology, saying that the twentieth century could be seen as the century of transformation thanks to feminism and the upheavals it had generated in social patterns.

Did she not recall Bergen-Belsen even once during that week, and therefore refrained from talking about it? She did mention her murdered mother and sisters, but in a painful context other than their death—that of her childhood. I had always assumed that Bergen-Belsen or Auschwitz—for her and for others—was a memory that is non-memory, namely ever-present as a counterpoint to immediate thinking and speaking, inevitably and constantly resurfacing. I was proven wrong—both about her and about my father, who also refrained from mentioning Auschwitz. Perhaps because each of their respective Auschwitzes was so present, it was not recalled. Or recalled but still sparing me? Her whole lifetime she tended not to spare me. I mean, she spared me no harsh thoughts or painful memories (although now I realize how many she avoided and how many questions I missed). So why spare me on her deathbed, which she recognized full well?

"Are you scared?" she asked me, eyes open wide, startled and curious in her hospital bed. Her motherly concern for me mixed with her own fear of the end.

The evening before I took her to the hospital, she said to me, sitting in her "Voltaire" easy chair, "Just you wait, I'll recover a bit and tell you what it's like to die." I laughed and cried. I could not protest and tell her she was not going to die. And I could not persuade her to speak—for the record—about "how it feels to die." I could not tell whether this was one of those conscious, jocular sparks she sometimes let out or an odd product of her confusion. Just like her words to the hospital doctors: One morning, as several doctors and interns gathered around her bed, she looked at them with distant curiosity. "What is this, a general assembly?" They burst into laughter and thought she was perfectly lucid. And she, I think, told me her opinion of doctors, but in Yugoslav that I had not learned. On her last day at the hospital, a doctor (a Palestinian who had studied in France, so they conversed in French) still tried to poke around her vein for some blood test. She observed him and his attempts with an anthropologist's distance. "All this hocus-pocus," she said, "just to keep me alive." He gave up trying.

We went back to her Motza nursing home with Tirza Waisel, who had come especially from London to be with Hanna. They met in the Tel Aviv feminist movement twenty-five years earlier. Their forty-six-year age difference notwithstanding, Hanna had become her soul mate and mentor. Thus Tirza was like a younger sister to me, sharing those last pains, and today she is perhaps the only person left besides me who misses Hanna and Abraham (who, separately, became her special counselor on matters of class and class struggle).

I was able to participate in the annual Women in Black demonstration on June 8, 2001, at Jerusalem's Paris Square. "Go on," Hanna urged me, when I told her I was leaving her for a while for that purpose. In the previous large demonstration of Women in Black—in December 2000, I believe—we still participated together. But this one I went to alone, after a terrible night of moaning and insomnia and muffled cries, from which I had escaped, leaving Tirza to stay with her. I leaned down to kiss her. She raised her head and looked up at me. From her Voltaire chair (in which her feet were sure to reach the floor and her back always straight): "Still that same blouse ..." she said in French.

Was she scolding me or making an anthropological observation? I had been in Ramallah when the doctor summoned me to her. I hadn't thought of a change of clothes....

I was at the demonstration when Tirza called, excited, to tell me that Hanna was sitting on the balcony, calm, and had even been fed a few teaspoonsful of ice cream.

I think Tirza was still hoping Hanna would recover. When I got back I found her there, her face very smooth, smiling lightly, enjoying the sun. I told her about the fairly large turnout at the demonstration, and she seemed very attentive as she remarked, "Great" (in Hebrew).

She had known enough demonstrations in her lifetime not to have illusions about the possible effect of one or even ten thousand such events. In the last eight months of her life—the first eight months of the Second Intifada—she suffered great pain both in body and in mind, and was distressed with what seemed to her a worthless existence.

So she did not quite realize how severe the situation had become, nor did she want to. Fortunately she was spared thoughts of forcibly collaborating with the herd that follows its bomb-throwing generals. She had told me several times in the past that she had made a mistake by immigrating to Israel. She also said this after returning from yet another "migration" of hers, a ten-year attempt at correcting a mistake. At the age of sixty-nine or seventy, in 1982 or 1983, she decided to move to France. I interpreted this as another one of her escapes. Ever since I was a little girl I remember her running away: to her study, to the Scottish Hospice in Jerusalem, later—when she received her pension from Yugoslavia—to travel in Europe, staying at cheap family hotels, riding trains (with her walking stick) to visit Moyra McCrory, an Irish writer in Liverpool whom I had known on the kibbutz, from there to London to visit feminist activists. The Sabra and Shatila massacre found her and my father in some anti-Nazi fighters' reunion in Europe, a communist organization that was a microcosm of contradictions, dreams, and lies. They packed up and hurried back to Israel, gave up their vacation plans. Several months later she packed her bags again and went to Paris. She characterized her escape streak with two jokes: A Jew—Romanian, say—wants to emigrate from Romania, so he goes to a travel agency. Israel? No. Too many wars (or Jews). The United States? Too capitalistic. The USSR? Are you out of your mind? South Africa? Racism over there is a bit much. Finally the Jew asks the travel agent, "Say, haven't you got another globe?" The second joke is about another Jew—say another Romanian—who immigrates to Israel. After a few months he misses Romania and goes back. This happens again and again. Somebody asks him, "Can't you make up your mind? Where do you feel best?" And he answers: "En route."

Not long ago I was asked whether it was true that after—and because of—the Sabra and Shatila massacre she resolved to leave Israel. My memory provides no answer. All I knew was that she wished to die abroad, to shift her personal history: to go back to the diaspora, to her a kind of homeland that had expelled her. Vanish there.

She came back to Israel in 1993, eighty years old, having almost obtained permanent resident status in France (or was it citizenship? I no longer remember). Suddenly she had discovered what a stranger she was there as well. I teased her: "You realized you won't die that easily, and remembered you have a daughter who will take care of you." But the escape option was always natural for her: "Don't you feel like leaving?" she tried to talk me into dropping everything and going away a few years ago, just when I felt more attached to the country than ever, through my living and working in Gaza and the West Bank.

Unlike her, Abraham felt attached to Israel. To the people, landscape, language, local politics. Not a Zionist attachment, rather that of a refugee who had escaped the void in his homeland, Romania, convinced that with "five years, ten at the most," he would help build socialism in that "other globe." The dream was his homeland. At the same time, he occasionally defined himself as a "guest" or "tourist" or "foreigner": at times he meant in Israel, at others in the world. He always bore the minority within him: once that of a Jew in anti-Semitic Romania, now that of a communist in a nationalist society, or of one who, in order to make a living, must sell cheaply his own efforts and energy in a capitalist world. Detached and bound at the same time.

He was connected to a feeding tube in the hospital. Sometimes he did not remember where he was. But, with a finger he could hardly raise anymore, he pointed to the tube that bothered him, and said, fifteen hours before he died, "Just like the Palestinian prisoners, when they were on their hunger strike" and were force-fed through tubes. I wrote about this in my book, *Drinking the Sea at Gaza*—he was the first reader of all my drafts and I kept telling him more details that he was eager to hear. So often he told me he could hardly bear the thought that at any given moment, some Palestinian prisoner in some dungeon is being tortured by an Israeli "Shabak" [General Security Services] interrogator.

Then, from the Palestinian prisoners, it was only natural for the associations of a dying man to revert to his own arrests, to what he wanted me to remember: "I was arrested (by the Israeli police) thirteen times (as a member and activist of the Israeli Communist Party)." (Or sixteen, now I no longer remember and curse my own reluctance to immediately write down his last phrases.) I knew: arrested for demonstrating against the military regime imposed on the Palestinian citizens of Israel (which lasted from 1948 to 1965), for distributing flyers against Ben-Gurion's policies, against the 1956 war that Israel fought with Britain and France against Egypt, for organizing workers' strikes. One of the stories I loved listening to as a young girl was about one of these arrests that lasted anywhere from a few hours to a day or two, and ended, as usual, without any indictment. They were simply a part of dissident life and a warning measure. ICP members' clear instructions were never to have their fingerprints taken by the police. After all, fingerprints are taken from criminals, not political activists. The police insisted on keeping him in custody until he would relent and have his prints taken. He was brought before a judge to extend custody. The judge scolded him for refusing. As the judge talked, my father removed the lace from of one of his orthopedic shoes. In the ghetto, at the age of nineteen or twenty, his toes had frozen. As a result, one foot was toeless and the other had only the first joint of each toe. He placed his toeless foot on the judge's table and said: "I have already had my fingerprints taken...." The judge let him go. My mind preserved this story with all the folktales—Romanian, Yugoslav, and Jewish—that my parents used to tell me as bedtime stories, where the weaker good guys eventually tricked the stronger bad guys....

But I was less heroic one evening in the early '60s, when policemen came to our home. They were looking for my mother. At noon she had distributed flyers against the Ben-Gurion government near Jerusalem's first supermarket. I was scared. The policemen conducted a search—I think it included my room as well—and we thought they had come to arrest her. She said to me aloud, "What are you afraid of? Haven't you learned in school that Jewish policemen are good?" Her calm cynicism must have reassured me without my realizing it.

Between 2001 and 2004, as a resident of Ramallah and a frequenter of the Gaza Strip, I personally experienced Israeli attacks against the Palestinian population. And while shrinking to the corner of a room in anticipation of a bombing blast, I always thought of my parents. Every time they heard Israeli fighter planes roaring overhead on their way to bombing targets, they cringed, their faces ashen. "We lived through that, we know what bombs are like," they said. They knew that within minutes an Israeli pilot would drop his payload over a refugee camp or a Beirut neighborhood, and loathed what they considered their own collaborative passivity as they sat on their kitchen porch. When Rehav'am Ze'evi prepared to run for Knesset with his own Moledet, a transferist party, in the latter half of the '80s, someone organized a rally for him at Tel Aviv University. Several leftist professors and students came in order to "do something." But they did not know what to do. When the moderator got up to introduce Ze'evi, and before he even finished his first sentence, Abraham—my father—stood up.

"I must address the protocol," he said. The moderator, out of sheer respect for the elderly, or perhaps amazement and lack of experience, let him speak. "Whoever told you it is legitimate to speak about transfer? This is not acceptable. You are discussing a forbidden subject." He had no inhibitions in this regard: anything connected to transfer—expulsion, murder, racist incitement of any sort—did not merit "freedom of speech and thought." He sounded more and more agitated. "I've already experienced fascism once. I have no strength to go through it again." It was the cue for those students and professors to do what they had to, namely, to break up the meeting.

In the background were always comparisons, made by leftists in Israel and abroad, between Israel and Nazi Germany. There

always were—and are—those who cannot help but compare anything Jews and Israel do with Nazism. It is a fashion that began
even before the First Intifada or the Second. We were of the same
mind, that those parallels were wrong and inappropriate, that
they were a disservice to the Palestinian struggle for liberation,
that more accurate historical parallels do exist, and that an oppressive regime need not resemble the German murder industry
for us to oppose it. Still, on one occasion, between newscasts during the First Intifada, Abraham said to me very painfully: "I don't
know what's worse anymore. True, we Jews were expelled and
murdered, but it lasted five years and came to an end. But I see
no end to the suffering we inflict on the Palestinians: 1948, then
exile, then 1967 and this unending Occupation." When Iraqi
missiles were launched, targeting Tel Aviv, acquaintances com-
plained to him about "Palestinians dancing on rooftops." He retorted with typical Yiddish irony, "Where else should they
dance? They are under curfew, so they can't quite dance in the
streets, now can they?" He thought it wouldn't do the Israelis any
harm to learn their own little lesson in fear, and identified with
that short happy outburst (politically short-lived) of people
gripped for years in the reign of terror and oppression by the Israeli occupier, and living under curfew for weeks and months on
end. How precisely he described for me life under curfew—even
without having traveled through the Occupied Territories.

At the hospital I asked him if he wanted me to inform his
family so they could say their farewells. One sister was a Gush

Emunim (Israeli colonist movement) sympathizer, and every rare meeting with her ended in a shouting match and fury that lasted for days. Two of his nephews are colonists of the "ideological" kind. Half-paralyzed, sometimes knowing where he was, other times not, holding and constantly caressing my hand in his right hand, he answered me unequivocally: "I don't want colonies in the hospital."

He was mortified with fear when I used to travel in my car to West Bank villages in the early '90s, as part of my work with Kav La'Oved (a workers' hotline, protecting Palestinian workers' rights). He explained his fears to me: "If they throw stones or shoot you, they have good reason." Hanna saw my activism and then my choice to live in the Occupied Territories as a more abstract issue, especially in the last few years, which enabled her not to worry about me. When she saw photos of Palestinian children and youths throwing stones at soldiers and other Occupation agents, she did not associate this with me. She always responded with her laconic all-purpose expression: "What sweethearts!" (in Yugoslav, *slatko*), not needing to repeat another banal slogan about rights, etc. She simply expressed her feelings contrary to those normally expressed by most Israelis about stone-throwing Palestinians. The right to fight the occupier inside occupied territory was natural, fundamental. "Had the ghetto been hermetically closed like Gaza," Abraham responded to my reports from the prison that Gaza became in the "Oslo peace years," after 1994, "we would not have survived." He, the youngest brother, sneaked out of the ghetto to work for Ukrainian farmers and brought home his daily wage: a sack of potatoes or the like.

One question about the ghetto; that was the only exception I allowed myself in my decision not to "stage" his dying. It was directly associated with his feeding tube. After he recalled the Palestinian prisoners and his own arrests, he thought of the Yarkon River: the event was that of the Makkabiya (a Jewish olympiad) disaster, where athletes, stepping on a collapsing bridge, fell into the polluted Yarkon River (whose delta Abraham could see from his home). Two victims died and others contracted strange pollution-induced illnesses, possibly from kerosene or oil in the river. "They might find kerosene in my body, as in the Yarkon," he said. From there his mind wandered to someone we knew several years earlier, a young man who once had lice, was too ashamed to mention it, and went ahead and bought kerosene in order to get rid of them. I am almost certain that at that moment I asked about lice in the ghetto, checking whether that would bring on some last remarks about the ghetto. I recalled a scene he once described for me: his father sitting by the table in a cellar crammed full with seven or eight family members, exhausted, hungry, and ill. The lice fell out of his beard and he sobbed for the first time.

But Abraham would not be tricked. He confirmed that he had had lice in the ghetto, and how humiliating that was, and that was as far as he went. If other recollections of the ghetto came up in those last hours of his life, he did not share them with me. In any case he was already sinking into ever-longer moments of absence, and his phrases were becoming less and less coherent.

The previous evening he had still minced his words. He said to me, "You have to show solidarity and get me out of here," namely, out of the hospital. In other words, not sentiment but rather action was needed. Naturally I could not get him out of the hospital. He refused all the nurses' pleas to use a bedpan as he lay in his hospital bed. "It will make things easier for you," I tried as well. "If I were ill you would be telling me the same thing." "You are still young," he answered. "You still pay taxes, you are still of use to the system. I am old, dispensable, and all I have left is my dignity." What could I do other than continue to stroke and kiss him, and have him stroke my head and hug me with his one good arm?

Just four days earlier we had met as usual in Tel Aviv. I would come to visit them regularly on weekends from Gaza, and then later from Ramallah. I no longer recall what in our conversation had suddenly conjured up for him the vineyards of the Palestinian villages on the way to Jerusalem. He remembered, still shocked, all the Israelis who—in the first summers following the Nakba*— raided the grapevines that went on growing even after their owners

---

* Arabic for "catastrophe." Nakba is how the Palestinians term the mass expulsion of some 700,000 people from their homes in the creation of the state of Israel during the 1948 war—the loss of their lands and property for the benefit of the new Jewish state, and the exile and the breaking up of the Palestinian community into several disconnected, debilitated communities, in Gaza, the West Bank, and Israel, and in many states of exile.

and planters and tenders had been expelled and made refugees. "I was stunned," he told me "at how unashamed they were."

I wondered. This was the first time he ever shared this memory with me. Over the years, I noticed, he had not accumulated specifics about the Nakba nor shared with me everything he knew. The contradictions were too painful, I suppose. He opened up more and more to the excruciating details when I had moved to Gaza, as I would always bring with me the stories of my refugee friends and sights of the refugee camps.

Once, in the early '90s, Abraham told me a dream of his. He dreamt it after we attended a concert together at Tel Aviv's Heichal Hatarbut (Philharmonic auditorium). He had received tickets from someone who was away. The First Intifada had come to an impasse, and it was difficult to keep count of the Palestinian lives lost and days under curfew. The audience in that concert hall luxuriated in its cultured finesse. In his dream, Abraham and I were standing on a hill, and people streamed from the east, covering the hills and valleys. "Amira'le, they are back, they are coming back!" he told me he had said in his dream, delighted, relieved.

But from the balcony of my mother's room in Motza, the line was drawn again between the dream and the possibility to undo history. A half-ruined stone structure partly covered with soil and growing thorns and weeds had already become an integral part of the hill across the way. In the early '90s I began to attach to the prickly pear cactus hedges and village ruins the names of more and more families I met—first in Gaza, then in the West Bank—who had come from there. Mustafa and Bassam are from Breir ("Bror Hayil"), Lama from Masmiya. And in Ramallah I made the acquaintance of Mohammad, collector of popular Palestinian music and musician (whose self-made flute at Ketziot prison had been confiscated) who came from Qalunia: the very village on whose land Mevaseret Yerushalayim and Maoz Zion were built, adjacent to Motza. (In 1859 Jews purchased land from Qalunia and began living there in the early twentieth century, I learned from the book *All That Remains* about the Palestinian villages that went to ruin).

In one of our last trips together to the Galilee, Hanna ordered me outright: "Just don't tell me everywhere what village had been there earlier." I couldn't resent this—because of her age, because of our desire to enjoy ourselves together for a while, because I realized that she, like my father, was living the contradiction that is inherent to Israel: a refugee state founded after the diaspora had expelled them, on the one hand, and on the other, being a state and society that expels. Certainly in the case of my parents, suppression was not meant to justify personal collaboration. In 1949, when they had just arrived in Israel, both my mother and father—separately, they had not yet met—rejected the Jewish Agency's offer to occupy for good, like many others, the emptied homes of refugees in Jerusalem. It was their gut feeling that as refugees themselves they could not possess a home of other refugees. A gut feeling that I bless to this day. For not having bestowed upon me an Arab house (code for a large, beautiful, expensive stone house) and an aesthetic-bourgeois dilemma in Jerusalem's Baq'a or Talbiya neighborhoods.

During Hanna's last day alive, when she no longer said a word or responded to my embraces and kisses, not even with a faint squeeze of the hand, I had no idea whether my mother registered anything said around her. The male nurse at the hospital said she was neither registering anything nor suffering. Emotionally I could not part from her, not explicitly, in words or declarations. On Saturday afternoon, June 9, 2001, my friend Michal Levin came to be with us. We sat on either side of her bed in the nursing ward of her home, not knowing what to do, what to say, whether to say anything at all. We decided to sing. It was not easy. Some songs had been forgotten, some childhood songs were inappropriate (as we now understood them to be nationalistic and belligerent), many others would have meant nothing to her. We sang her the song about the hyacinth that she had always loved and sang for me. I sang some French children's song she once taught me. I thought I noticed her smile faintly when I sang that French song, but didn't know whether it was my imagination or an actual smile. And then I sang "Avanti Popolo," which she had taught me in Italian. Michal knew the tune, not the lyrics. I repeated the song and translated it for her. The door was open. Nurses peered in at us curiously, and we went on singing. When we got to the words "*bandierra rossa*" (red flag), Hanna moved her lips and sang those two words along with us. At 9:00 a.m. the next morning, she died.

Amira Hass
Translated by Tal Haran

Yugoslav Worlds
of Hanna Lévy-Hass

Emil Kerenji

The one time I was laughed out of somebody's office did not ultimately affect my academic career, but I still remember the occasion very well. The year was 2001, and I was at the beginning of my Ph.D. studies in history at the University of Michigan. I wanted to write a dissertation about Yugoslav Jews after the Holocaust, but my ideas at the time were vague and undifferentiated. When I told a professor—who, thankfully, did not end up sitting on my dissertation committee—that I wanted to work on Yugoslav Jews, he burst out into uncontrollable laughter: Yugoslav Jews! That doesn't exist! Are you a "Yugoslav Jew" (I could feel the heavy scare quotes in the air)? With that name—Kerenji?

That was a fair point. "Experts" on things East European usually immediately recognize my name as "Hungarian," and not infrequently I get complimented on how fluently I speak my own mother tongue—a language that officially used to be called

"Serbo-Croatian, that is, Croato-Serbian" when I went to elementary school in Novi Sad, in the Yugoslav province of Vojvodina, in the early 1980s. Today, in post-Yugoslav Novi Sad, the language is called "Serbian"; and in Hanna Lévy-Hass's native Sarajevo, children go to school and learn "Bosnian" language and literature. We learn from Amira Hass that her mother referred to the language as "Yugoslav"; but in addition to revealing Hanna's commitment to Yugoslav utopia and, as the flip side of this commitment, her acceptance of the political marginality of this position—which was as marginal, I should point out, during much of the period of Socialist Yugoslavia as it is today—this appellation reveals a larger truth about the delicate connection of Yugoslav Jewishness to the Yugoslav political project.

For the Jews of the South Slav lands, the "Yugoslav" language became the "language of community," to borrow the phrase from Hillel Kieval, who studied similar processes in the Czech context.[1] Like Yugoslavia, Yugoslav Jewishness was a political project. It was first imagined as a possibility towards the end of the nineteenth century, when a group of Jewish "Yugoslav"-speaking students in Vienna, electrified by the agitation of the prophets of Zionism, Herzl and Nordau, which dominated Central European middle-class Jewish debates of the *fin de siècle*, started seeing themselves as leaders of a unified, politically conscious, "national" Jewish community. Being in Vienna at the time, and attending talks in overflowing university amphitheaters in which fired-up students raged about a Jewish state and a new, Hebrew culture, must have intoxicated a handful of provincial students who came from the Balkans and spoke a strange mix of south Slavic dialects. Most of them were from towns in Croatia and Slavonia—mostly Zagreb and Slavonski Brod—but several came from Sarajevo, and even Belgrade.

Having converted to Zionism, they considered themselves the political *avant-garde* of the Jewish community in the lands from which they came. The only problem was that this imagined community did not exist—a problem most nineteenth-century nationalists were bound to face at some point—and that, more importantly, Jews who were imagined to belong to it were utterly disinterested in this kind of belonging. So when these Viennese students returned to their hometowns for the summer holidays, they were annoyed to find out that few of their compatriots had ever heard of Herzl, and that fewer still were interested in caring about Jews in other south Slav lands.

There were good reasons for this lack of interest. The lands that would end up comprising the first Yugoslav state in the aftermath of World War I were politically divided—moreover, they lacked any semblance of a common past—and Jewish communities populating them were extremely diverse. Native lands of most of the members of *Bar Giora*—the name of the "society of Jewish academics from the Yugoslav lands" that these students founded in 1902—lay in the southern provinces of Austria-Hungary (Croatia, Slavonia, and Bosnia-Hercegovina); some members came from Serbia, a former Ottoman territory that had first won autonomy in the first half of the nineteenth century, and then independence by 1878;

and "Jews from the Yugoslav lands" in the view of the Zionists from *Bar Giora*, encompassed all these territories, including what is today Macedonia, which, at the time, was still under Ottoman rule. Not only was this "Yugoslav" landscape thus crisscrossed by fairly fortified political boundaries—which, in the case of Serbia's and Austria-Hungary's Bosnian border, separated enemy states, deeply suspicious of one another's intentions—but the Jewish communities in these lands mainly considered themselves parts of larger communities whose centers lay far beyond the "Yugoslav" lands. The German-speaking middle class Jews of Croatia were not sure that they had anything in common with Hungarian-speaking Jews of Slavonia; but if this link was questionable, what then to say of the Bosnian Ladino-speaking Sephardim, steeped in Ottoman Jewish culture, impoverished and dismissive of well-fed Ashkenazi intruders who started settling in Bosnia after the province was taken from the Ottoman Empire and forcibly put under Austrian rule in 1878? And what to make of the fervently nationalistic "Serbs of Mosaic faith" in Serbia, who, like most Serbs, despised Austria-Hungary and, most of all, its Jews, whom they saw as *par excellence* agents of its effeminate Western civilization?

Early Zionist work in the "Yugoslav" lands was, therefore, not at all easy. Persuading Ashkenazim from Zagreb that they had anything in common with Sephardim from Sarajevo—let alone with Sephardim from Serbia—was an uphill battle. But despite all the differences among the Jewish populations of the "Yugoslav" lands, what was increasingly going to bind them together, the

Zionists understood correctly, was their "Yugoslav" language. New generations of Jews were becoming bilingual, and along with their traditional first languages—German, Hungarian, Ladino, and Yiddish—they increasingly spoke fluent "Yugoslav," in its regional variants. In Serbia, it was called "Serbian," in Croatia, "Croatian"; but whatever the appellation, because of the strategic decision of Serbian and Croatian elites to standardize the language in the first half of the nineteenth century, this was the tongue that diverse populations, non-Jewish and Jewish alike, from northern Adriatic to southeastern Serbia could now understand, and a variant of which they now used on a daily basis.[2]

Imagining Yugoslav Jewishness, therefore, became inseparable from this *lingua franca* of the Western Balkans; and political organization of Yugoslav Jews, in turn, became inseparable from Zionism. "Yugoslav," thus, became the new language of Zionism. It is ironic that, while most Zionists elsewhere were twisting their tongues trying to learn Hebrew, the language of Jewish rebirth, Zionists in the Balkans were struggling to master the language of Balkan Slavs. This often assumed grotesque proportions: in 1904, at the "First Public Congress of Jewish Academics from the Yugoslav Lands," held strategically in Osijek, one of the easternmost Jewish centers of Austro-Hungarian Slavonia (and thus closest to the Serbian capital, Belgrade), speakers addressed the audience in "Croatian" or "Serbian"; but the butchered address of one Otto Kraus was so insufferable that the panelists asked him repeatedly to switch to his native German—which, needless to say, he refused.[3] There were high stakes in adopting this language; and one could not be a proper Zionist without mastering it.

The first Jewish periodicals in the Balkans that looked beyond the parochial communities of German-, Ladino-, Yiddish-, or Hungarian speakers were thus published in "Yugoslav," and were staunchly Zionist. The use of language of these publications—first *Židovska smotra* [*The Jewish Review*], and, later, *Židov* [*The Jew*]—reflected the linguistic heterogeneity of "Yugoslav"-speaking Jewish communities of the Balkans. Texts were published in whatever dialect of the language the contributors had originally written it, from Serbian Cyrillic to Serbian, Croatian, and Bosnian variants written in Roman script. On the eve of World War I, a tenuous reading public had emerged, a Jewish readership across the Balkans, ready to view itself as a culturally heterogeneous, yet distinctly "Yugoslav" Jewish community with common political interests.

II.

It was into this political and linguistic context that Hanna Lévy-Hass was born in Sarajevo, the capital of Bosnia-Hercegovina, in 1913. Her parents spoke Ladino; but Hanna, her daughter tells us, spoke "Yugoslav." Her choice of language was illustrative of the shift that had occurred from the generation of *Bar Giora* to the next one: Jews now spoke the language of other south Slavs, and increasingly communicated in it both with other Jews and their non-Jewish compatriots.

Although, as we have seen, "Yugoslav" had initially been the language of Zionism, once the Yugoslav Jewish public sphere was established, it became contested by various different political groups. Hanna Lévy-Hass's Sarajevo, for example, was home of the staunchly Sephardist newspaper, *Jevrejski glas* [*Jewish Voice*], which vehemently opposed the Zagreb-based Union of Zionists of Yugoslavia, and their criticisms of alleged Sephardi backwardness and lack of political consciousness. But the wages of linguistic proficiency in the majority language did not affect just the sphere of Jewish politics; for the first time, there matured a viable generation of Jews—more numerous than their Zionist predecessors, whose Yugoslav choice, as it were, had been an exception, rather than a rule—who were either disinterested in Jewishness altogether (which was relatively painless in the Yugoslav ethnic mosaic), or were attracted by other political ideologies.

In Bosnia-Hercegovina, more than in any other region of the Kingdom, it was the Communist movement that appealed the most to the new generation of Jewish youth. This was mainly due to the social profile of the Sephardi Jewish community in Bosnia-Hercegovina: unlike in other former parts of Austria-Hungary, where predominantly Ashkenazi Jews had gone through the process of embourgeoisement in the last quarter of the nineteenth century, and where their occupational structure overwhelmingly consisted of trade, industry, civil service, and free professions, a significant portion of Sephardim of Bosnia-Hercegovina (and, to a lesser extent, Serbia) were artisans and workers, and many were poor. The (banned) Communist Party of Yugoslavia—the only party in the interwar period that sought to forge a pan-Yugoslav political movement—thus appealed to many Jews.[4] *Matatya*, a Sarajevo Jewish youth organization, founded in 1923, was a clearinghouse for Jewish workers' activism, and a point through which close contact was maintained with the Communist Party of Yugoslavia, and its youth movement, Young Communist League of Yugoslavia.

Many Jews of Yugoslavia were members of the Communist Party; some were very prominent, like Moša Pijade, a Belgrade Sephardi Jew who, despite impeccable Communist credentials, until the end of his life in 1957 considered himself a Serb. Pijade's translation of *Das Kapital* is still the standard translation in Serbian; and from the early days of the Communist Party of Yugoslavia, Pijade served on its Executive Committee—when he was not in jail, in which he spent fourteen years of the short interwar period. Another indication of the appeal of the Communist Party to the Jews was the impressive number of Yugoslav Jews who volunteered to join the International Brigades to defend the Spanish Republic during the Civil War. For Sephardim from Bosnia and Serbia, fighting for the progressive Spanish Republic had an additional historical significance: their ancestors had been expelled from the Iberian peninsula in the late fifteenth century, and now a new, tolerant Spain, their distant motherland, was fighting its own historical demons personified by the clerical phalanxes of Francisco Franco and his allies, Fascist Italy and Nazi Germany.

All these coordinates characterized Hanna Lévy-Hass's teenage years and early adulthood. If it was certainly not inevitable, it was probably a part of a larger historical pattern that she should be drawn to the Communist movement in Yugoslavia. In that sense, her choice to study at the University of Belgrade was by no means arbitrary: in the early 1930s, when she started her studies in the Yugoslav capital, the University was dominated by Communist youth, and was one of the few progressive spaces in the country. Disproportionate numbers of Jews were enrolled as students at the University of Belgrade in that period, and many were affiliated with secret Communist Party cells. It was also in the halls of the University of Belgrade that the Communist youth fought it out—sometimes literally, with fists and iron bars—with Serbian Fascists, bands organized by Dimitrije Ljotić, who would later, during the Nazi occupation of Serbia from 1941 to 1944, organize the Serbian quisling military guard and openly collaborate with the Nazis in suppressing the Communist-led insurrection and rounding up and exterminating Serbian Jews.

As Hanna Lévy-Hass was beginning her studies in Belgrade, the country was drawing ever closer to Axis powers. Because of Italian and Hungarian revisionism—Serbia, as one of the victorious Allies in World War I, secured for the new state most of the Adriatic coast, traditionally claimed by Italy, and a former part of Hungary north of the Sava and Danube rivers—Yugoslavia's foreign policy was very careful in the interwar years. However, by the mid-1930s, German and Italian economic hegemony had fateful consequences for foreign policies of all Central European countries, and Yugoslavia was no exception. By 1940, pressured by Nazi Germany, which, after the 1938 *Anschluß*, was now Yugoslavia's neighbor, Yugoslavia introduced two anti-Jewish laws—one limiting Jewish enrollment at universities, and one banning Jews from dealing in food products. On March 25, 1941, Yugoslavia formally joined Hitler's Tripartite Pact. Two days later, however, a group of pro-British army officers seized power in Belgrade, triggering mass anti-German demonstrations in the capital. Hitler was furious; ten days later, on April 6, 1941, Nazi Germany and its allies invaded Yugoslavia.

World War II in Yugoslavia was a complex web of interrelated civil wars, genocidal policies, occupations, partitions, and new patron-client relationships. The country was overrun in a mere twelve days, amidst general demoralization and mass desertion. Serbia and Banat were occupied by the *Wehrmacht*; a few months later, Milan Nedić became prime minister of a collaborationist government in Serbia, which acted as a Nazi bulwark against Communist insurrection and a facilitator of the plan for the extermination of the Jews. An "Independent State of Croatia" (known as NDH, *Nezavisna država Hrvatska*), a Nazi puppet state run by the genocidal *ustaša* regime led by Ante Pavelić, was proclaimed on the territory of Croatia, Slavonia, Dalmatia, and Bosnia-Hercegovina, with Italian and German troops occupying their respective spheres of interest. Slovenia was partitioned, its parts annexed by the Nazi Reich and Mussolini's Italy. Parts of Kosovo and Montenegro were occupied by Italy, while Macedonia was annexed by Bulgaria and Bačka by Hungary. In April 1941, Yugoslavia ceased to exist.

The fate of the Jews, although everywhere tragic, depended on the territory in which they found themselves in this arbitrary partition; new administrative lines determined who was to live and who was to die, and when. Serbian Jews were murdered already by the spring of 1942, by shooting and gas. In Croatia, the mass murder of the Jews was initially put on the back burner, as the genocide against the Serbs was a more pressing task for the *ustaša* regime, but was in full swing already in the summer of 1941. Macedonian Jews under Bulgarian occupation were deported to Treblinka in March 1943, while the Jews of Bačka were rounded up by Hungarians and deported to Auschwitz in the summer of 1944. In Italian-occupied areas, however, anti-Jewish policy was much less strict, and many Jews were able to survive by staying in or fleeing to those areas—Dalmatia, parts of Montenegro and Kosovo—and later, after the capitulation of Italy in 1943, joining the Yugoslav partisans. Of the about 75,000 Jews of Yugoslavia on the eve of World War II, about 15,000 survived the war.

Most survived by joining the multiethnic, Communist-led Movement for National Liberation. Led by the charismatic Secretary General of the Communist Party of Yugoslavia, a Croat Josip Broz, known as Tito, this was the only genuine resistance movement in the country, and the only political option that was not antisemitic. It was also the only political movement that still regarded Yugoslavia as a relevant political framework, and which fought for the liberation of the entire country and the establishment of a federation of equal Yugoslav nations and national minorities. All this, of course, was appealing to the Jews, who could either join a resistance movement that genuinely accepted them as Jews—a virtual impossibility almost anywhere else in Nazi-occupied Europe—or risk almost certain death. Of course, it is possible to imagine antisemitic incidents in Tito's motley army, mostly consisting, as it did, of peasants and workers of all Yugoslav nationalities, many of whom were certainly not emancipated, and certainly not free from anti-Jewish prejudice. At the levels of ideology, official rhetoric and the circle of leadership, however, the movement was not only not anti-semitic, but it also referenced specifically, already during the war, the mass murder of Jews perpetrated by "occupiers and domestic traitors," as the phrase went, as one of the crimes against the peoples of Yugoslavia, for which they (the occupiers and the traitors) would have to face justice after the war.

It is thus easy to see how joining the partisans would have appealed to Hanna Lévy-Hass—as a Jew, but also as a politically aware woman. Until 1943, she stayed in Italian-occupied Montenegro, and occasionally took part in the actions of the partisans. But when the Germans took over in 1943, the final decision not to go—for fear of German retaliation against other Jews, as Amira Hass relates—sealed her fate. She was arrested by the *Gestapo*, and eventually deported to Bergen-Belsen.

III.

The unfortunate fact about the text of Hanna Lévy-Hass's diary is that it is a translation from the French; the original, written in her native "Yugoslav," has so far not been found.

The translation itself is excellent, and it is much better than the first, 1982 English edition. Although Hanna Lévy-Hass herself translated the original text into French, in which she was fluent, only through the original would one of the most important themes of her diary fully come through: her absolute and unassailable conviction, amidst terrible suffering and uncertainty that she would survive, that a Socialist Yugoslavia was a viable option, and the best solution for the peoples of Yugoslavia. Even in the direst of circumstances, she found the strength to be a political human being. It is very difficult to write anything that does not ring hollow about a woman mustering her last atoms of strength to keep a diary in a Nazi camp in the mid-1940s, and I prefer to let the reader engage with the text on her own. It is not surprising, however, that Yugoslavia as a concept and as a hope occupies such an important place in the text. And yet once she was back in Belgrade after all this suffering, Hanna Lévy-Hass soon decided that her Yugoslavia was not really for her. In December 1948, she arrived in Haifa and became an Israeli—something she, as far as we know, never had any interest in becoming.

Why did she emigrate to Israel? She was not the only one: many non-Zionist Jews had made the same decision and left the country in the first wave of emigration from Yugoslavia in 1948. Amira Hass rightly points out the chasm that separated non-Jewish Yugoslav survivors of the Yugoslav catastrophe and the Jewish Yugoslav survivors of the Holocaust. The founding narrative in which the Communists, led by Tito, legitimized their new rule was the story of the "struggle for national liberation," and it was heroism, and not victimhood and suffering, that was foregrounded and celebrated. The new Yugoslav leadership had no time for mourning Jewish victims and pondering the magnitude of the Jewish catastrophe; although there is no way of knowing for sure, we can imagine that, upon return, Hanna Lévy-Hass tried to publish her diary in Yugoslavia, without success. (It remains unpublished in any of the Yugoslav successor states to this day.)

In the early 1950s, this changed: in order to differentiate its policies from those of the Soviet Union and its satellites, with which it had broken off relations in 1948, Tito's Yugoslavia reached for the Holocaust and Jewish suffering. In 1952, the Federation of Jewish Communities of Yugoslavia published a volume entitled "Crimes of Fascist Occupiers and their Helpers against the Jews in Yugoslavia," and followed it up with a high-profile campaign of dedicating five monuments, at different sites in Yugoslavia, to "Jewish victims of Fascism."[5] A reviewer of the volume on the crimes against the Jews, writing in the journal published by the Yugoslav Ministry of Foreign Affairs in 1953, barely two months after the sentences had been handed down in the

Slánský trial in Czechoslovakia, pointed out that

> the book represents an invaluable historical document, a monument to the dark age of Hitlerite medieval vandalism.... It is the indictment ... not only of Hitlerite darkness ... but also of new dark forces, whether they be the old forces of Fascism rearing their ugly head in West Germany ... or their brethren in the USSR and its satellites, where a new witch hunt is waged, by well-tested infamous Hitlerite methods, against those same innocent Jews, decimated in the last war.[6]

Yugoslavia legitimized its new existence between East and West by pointing, as it were, to the fact that it cared about Jewish suffering, and that its Jews were fully integrated into society and supported the Yugoslav political project led by Tito (which was, by that time, largely true). To be Jewish in Yugoslavia, then, meant to be a Yugoslav without reservation, a person equal to all other Yugoslavs regardless of their background, while, in theory, preserving the Jewish historical heritage. This was an ambiguous gambit, one that, however, mostly worked until the mid-1980s.

In 1948, however, all this lay in the future. Upon her return from Bergen-Belsen, Hanna Lévy-Hass encountered in Belgrade both the wall of silence that she did not know how to tear down, and accusatory looks that greeted Jewish Holocaust survivors everywhere in Europe—"Are you still alive?" It was the dark shadow of this unspoken question that finally dissuaded her from ever settling down in Yugoslavia again, even in the late 1980s.

And perhaps it was for the best: when she came to her native land for the last time, it was ready to explode again, this time without Hitler and external aggression.

---

1. Hillel Kieval, *Languages of Community: The Jewish Experience in the Czech Lands* (Berkeley: University of California Press, 2000).
2. For a brief overview of the history of Serbo-Croatian linguistic unity in the nineteenth century, see Andrew Baruch Wachtel, *Making a Nation, Breaking a Nation: Literature and Cultural Politics in Yugoslavia* (Stanford: Stanford University Press, 1998), 24-31.
3. Ljiljana Dobrovšak, "Prvi cionisti ki kongres u Osijeku 1904. godine," *Časopis za suvremenu povijest*, Vol. 37, No. 2 (2005), 479-495.
4. Jaša Romano, *Jevreji Jugoslavije, 1941-1945: Žrtve genocida i učesnici Narodnooslobodilačkog rata* (Belgrade: Savez jevrejskih opština Jugoslavije, 1980), 40.
5. Zdenko Levental (ed.), *Zločini fašističkih okupatora i njihovih pomagača protiv Jevreja u Jugoslaviji* (Belgrade: Savez jevrejskih opština Jugoslavije, 1952).
6. Vera Nikolova, "Zlo ini fašisti kih okupatora i njihovih pomaga a protiv Jevreja u Jugoslaviji," *Međunarodni problemi*, Vol. 5, No. 1 (January-March 1953), 128-130, 128.

In Praise of Barbarians: Essays Against Empire
Mike Davis • No writer in the United States today brings together analysis and history as comprehensively and elegantly as Mike Davis. In these contemporary, interventionist essays, Davis goes beyond critique to offer real solutions and concrete possibilities for change. ISBN: 9781931859424

Between the Lines: Readings on Israel, the Palestinians, and the U.S. "War on Terror"
Tikva Honig-Parnass and Toufic Haddad • This compilation of essays—edited by a Palestinian and an Israeli—constitutes a challenge to critically rethink the Israeli-Palestinian conflict. ISBN 9781931859448

Poetry and Protest: A Dennis Brutus Readers
Dennis Brutus, edited by Aisha Karim and Lee Sustar • Dennis Brutus, imprisoned along with Nelson Mandela, is known worldwide for his unparalleled eloquence as an opponent of apartheid in South African. This vital collection of interviews, poetry, and essays brings together the full, forceful range of his work. ISBN: 9781931859226

Exile: Conversations with Pramoedya Ananta Toer
Andre Vltchek, Rosie Indira, edited by Nagesh Rao • Collected conversations with famed Indonesian writer, Pramoedya Ananta Toer. Exiled for ten years on the Buru Island internment camp, he is the author of the widely acclaimed "Buru quartet." ISBN: 9781931859288

ABOUT HAYMARKET BOOKS

Haymarket Books is a nonprofit, progressive book distributor and publisher, a project of the Center for Economic Research and Social Change. We believe that activists need to take ideas, history, and politics into the many struggles for social justice today. Learning the lessons of past victories, as well as defeats, can arm a new generation of fighters for a better world. As Karl Marx said, "The philosophers have merely interpreted the world; the point however is to change it."

We take inspiration and courage from our namesakes, the Haymarket Martyrs, who gave their lives fighting for a better world. Their 1886 struggle for the eight-hour day, which gave us May Day, the international workers' holiday, reminds workers around the world that ordinary people can organize and struggle for their own liberation. These struggles continue today across the globe—struggles against oppression, exploitation, hunger, and poverty.

It was August Spies, one of the Martyrs targeted for being an immigrant and an anarchist, who predicted the battles being fought to this day. "If you think that by hanging us you can stamp out the labor movement," Spies told the judge, "then hang us. Here you will tread upon a spark, but here, and there, and behind you, and in front of you, and everywhere, the flames will blaze up. It is a subterranean fire. You cannot put it out. The ground is on fire upon which you stand."

We could not succeed in our publishing efforts without the generous financial support of our readers. Many people contribute to our project through the Haymarket Sustainers program, where donors receive free books in return for their monetary support. If you would like to be a part of this program, please contact us at info@haymarketbooks.org.

Shop our full catalog online at www.haymarketbooks.org or call 773-583-7884.